CASS LIBRARY OF WEST INDIAN STUDIES
No. 10

A DESCRIPTION OF
BRITISH GUIANA

A DESCRIPTION

OF

BRITISH GUIANA

GEOGRAPHICAL AND STATISTICAL

Exhibiting its Resources and Capabilities

together with

The Present and Future Condition and
Prospects of the Colony

BY

ROBERT H. SCHOMBURGK

LONDON AND NEW YORK

First published 1840 by
FRANK CASS AND COMPANY LIMITED

Published 2013 by Routledge
2 Park Square, Milton Park, Abingdon, Oxfordshire OX14 4RN
711 Third Avenue, New York, NY, 10017

First issued in paperback 2014

Routledge is an imprint of the Taylor & Francis Group, an informa business

ISBN 13: 978-0-714-61949-1 (hbk)
ISBN 13: 978-1-138-01108-3 (pbk)

A DESCRIPTION

OF

BRITISH GUIANA,

GEOGRAPHICAL AND STATISTICAL:

EXHIBITING

ITS RESOURCES AND CAPABILITIES,

TOGETHER WITH

THE PRESENT AND FUTURE CONDITION AND PROSPECTS
OF THE COLONY.

BY

ROBERT H. SCHOMBURGK, Esq.

LONDON:
SIMPKIN, MARSHALL, AND CO.,
STATIONERS' HALL COURT.

1840.

THE object of the present work is to give an account of whatever relates to the physical structure, natural productions, and present and future capabilities of the colony of British Guiana, including the statistical information I have been able to procure. The result of my personal examinations in the course of my expeditions of discovery during successive years from 1835 to 1839, is offered in a spirit of strict impartiality. The pursuit of science alone led me to Guiana, and if by my statements of facts the interest of the province, as a British colony, is advanced, my object is attained.

Though the accompanying map is incomplete, many of its details resting on information procured from the natives, yet the greater portion has been laid down from my own personal observations, and offers a correct view of the facilities which the numerous rivers and their tributaries afford for internal navigation, and will show how important it is to the colony that its boundaries should be more clearly defined than at present, and freed from the encroaching claims of the adjacent states, which, if admitted, would deprive British Guiana of the greater part of her most valuable territory.

ROBERT H. SCHOMBURGK.

London, May 1840.

CONTENTS.

I.

GEOGRAPHICAL DESCRIPTION	1
Physical Aspect of the Colony	3
Geology	7
Rivers	11
Climate	17
Vegetable Productions	28
Animal Kingdom	37
Statistics of British Guiana	41
Inhabitants	42
Religious and Public Instruction	52
Public Income and Expenditure	57
Staple Products and Commerce	60
Form of Government, Civil Constitution, &c., of the Colony	69
Towns and Villages	73
Brief Historical Records of the present Colony of British Guiana	81

II.

RESOURCES AND CAPABILITIES OF BRITISH GUIANA 88

III.

THE PRESENT CONDITION AND FUTURE PROSPECTS OF THE COLONY 118

DESCRIPTION OF GUIANA.

I.

GEOGRAPHICAL DESCRIPTION.

GUIANA[*], Guyana, Guayana, or Guianna, is that part of South America which lies between 8° 40′ N. lat. and 3° 30′ S. lat. and the 50th and 68th degree of longitude, west of Greenwich. It is bounded on the north by the Atlantic and the eastern course of the river Orinoco, on the east likewise by the Atlantic, on the south by the rivers Negro and Amazon, on the west by the northern course of the Orinoco, the natural canal of Cassiquiare, and the southern course of the Rio Negro. Its greatest extent between

[*] The British portion is called Guiana in official documents; Guayana is the Spanish name, Guianna the Portuguese. The earliest Dutch settlers called it Guiana, or the wild coast. It is said to have received its name from a small river, a tributary of the Orinoco.

Cape North, and the confluence of the Rio Xie with the Rio Negro, is 1090 geogr. miles; its greatest breadth between Punta Barima, at the mouth of the Orinoco, to the confluence of the Rio Negro with the Amazon, 710 geogr. miles. Its line of sea-coast extends between the Amazon and the Orinoco, and is divided into Brazilian, French, Dutch, British, and Venezuelan Guiana, but its definite limits have never been obtained. All that has hitherto been done, between Spain, Portugal, and France, is regarded as only provisional, and the boundary which separates the British settlements from Venezuela and Brazil has never been determined.

British Guiana, undetermined state of its boundaries.

The following description is limited to those parts which comprehend British Guiana; but the exact knowledge of its area depends upon the determination of its boundaries; and in the uncertainty whether the pretensions of the Brazilian and Venezuelan governments will be attended to, it is impossible to come to a result. Some modern geographers extend British Guiana from the mouth of the Corentyn in 56° 58′ W. long. to Punta Barima in 60° 6′ W. long.; in consequence of the early Dutch settlers having had occupation of the eastern bank of the river Barima, where they had constructed a military outpost, before the English in 1666 had destroyed the fort of New Zealand, or New Middleburgh. The Republic of Venezuela claims the country to the mouth of the river Morocco, from thence to the confluence of the rivers Cuyuni and Mazaruni, along the western bank of the river Essequibo, to the confluence of the river Rupununi.

Area.

The Brazilians having lately claimed as far north as the mouth of the Siparunus, its area would then be reduced to about 12,300 square miles, and it would form the smallest of the three colonies in Guiana, which are possessed by European powers*. If we follow the limits which nature prescribes by its rivers and mountains, and include all the regions which are drained by the streams which fall into the Essequibo within the British territory, and adopting the river Corentyn as its eastern boundary, the counties Demerara, Essequibo, and Berbice, which constitute British Guiana, consist of 76,000 square miles.

Physical Aspect of the Colony.

Coast regions.

The banks and low lands adjacent to the chief rivers of British Guiana, namely the Essequibo, Demerara, Berbice, and Corentyn, consist of a blue clay, impregnated with marine salt mixed with decayed vegetable matter, which in its decomposed state forms rich mould and is highly productive. This alluvial flat extends from ten to twenty, and in some instances (as between the rivers Berbice and Corentyn,) even to forty miles inland, and is terminated by a range of sand-hills, from about 30 to 120 feet high, which approach the sea within two miles of the Arabisi coast of the Essequibo; if we follow them upwards from that point, they take first a S.E. by S., and afterwards a S.E. direction, traversing the whole colony. Almost parallel with the ridge of sand-hills run several detached groups of hillocks, of moderate elevation, being seldom more than 200 feet high; they cross the river Essequibo at Osterbecke Point, in lat. 6° 15' N., the Demerara at Arobaya, in 6° 5', the Berbice in 5°.

Sand hills and hillocks.

In the fifth parallel of latitude a chain of mountains is met with, which consists of granite, gneiss, and trappean

Mountains

* It is called the smallest European colony in Guiana, in the Dictionnaire Géographique Universel, Paris, 1828, vol. iv. p. 615, where the area is stated to consist only of 3120 leagues.

rocks, and their various modifications; they are an offset of the Orinoco mountains, with which they are connected by the Sierra Ussipama of geographers; they traverse Guiana in a south-eastern direction, and may be considered the central ridge of the colony. Whenever this chain crosses any of the rivers which have been under my investigation, it forms large cataracts, namely, those of Twasiniki and Ouropocari in the Essequibo, Itabrou and the Christmas cataracts in the river Berbice, and the great cataracts in the river Corentyn. The highest peak appear to be the mountains of St. George, at the Mazaruni, the Twasinki, and Maccari on the Essequibo (the latter rising about 1100 feet above the river), and the mountains of Itabrou, on the river Berbice, the highest of which, according to my barometrical admeasurement, was 662 feet above the river, and 828 feet above the sea. This chain appears to be connected with the Sierra Acarai by the Marowini mountains, and I am inclined to consider it the old boundary of the Atlantic, the geological features of the chain conducing to such a supposition. Further north commence hillocks of a lower elevation, and those ridges of sand the consequence of a retreating sea.

Pacaraima mountains. The mountains of Pacaraima approach the Essequibo in lat. 4° N., and are an offset of the Sierra Parima; their general direction is east and west, and as far as I have been able to ascertain, they consist only of primitive formation.

Roraima. The culminating point of this chain is a range of sandstone mountains, of which the highest is called Roraima by the Indians, in lat. 5° 9′ 30″ N., long. 60° 47′ W. This remarkable mountain group extends twenty-five miles in a north-west and south-east direction, and rises to 5000 feet above the table-land, or 7500 feet above the sea;

the upper 1500 feet presenting a mural precipice, more striking than I have ever seen elsewhere. Down the face of these mountains rush numerous cascades, which eventually form tributaries to the three great rivers of the northern half of South America; namely, the Amazon, the Orinoco, and the Essequibo. These mountains form the separation of waters of the basins of the Orinoco and Essequibo on the north, and the Amazon on the south, and they are therefore of the greatest importance in deciding the boundary of British Guiana.

The mountain Makarapan was formerly considered the highest point in Guiana, before I visited the Roraima mountains. This mountain approaches the river Rupununi in 3° 50′ N. lat., and rises to a height of about 3500 feet above the sea. *Makarapan.*

The Cannucu or Conocon mountains, in 3° N. lat., connect the Pacaraima mountains with the Sierra Acarai, in which the largest river of Guiana, the Essequibo, has its sources. The Acarai mountains likewise give rise to the river Corentyn, and form the southern boundary of British Guiana. I shall designate them as the mountains of the equator, that imaginary line cutting their axis. They are densely wooded, and display the vigorous and luxuriant vegetation which is the striking feature of Guiana. These mountains do not reach the height of the Roraima; I estimated the highest at about 4000 feet. The Ouangouwai, or Mountains of the Sun, form the connecting link between the Acarai and Carawaimi mountains; the Tarapona mountains between the latter and the Cannucu and Pacaraima mountains. *Cannucu and Acarai Mountains.*

A peculiar feature of British Guiana are the savannahs, which extend between the rivers Demerara and Corentyn, and approach the sea-shore at the river Berbice. They are not directly connected with the great savannahs of *Savannahs.*

the Rupununi, as the second ridge of mountains intervenes. These great savannahs are encompassed by the Sierra Pacaraima to the north, the Cannucu, Taripona, and Carawaimi mountains to the south, the thick forests of the Essequibo and isolated mountains to the east, and the mountains of the Mocajahi, and offsets of the Sierra Parima to the west*. The winding course of the rivers are generally marked with fringes of trees; and, if we except in some places tufts of trees which rise like verdant isles or oases in a desert from amidst these plains, they are merely covered with grasses and a few stunted trees.

These Savannahs are the probable site of the lake Parima and El Dorado.

The geological structure of this region leaves but little doubt that it was once the bed of an inland lake, which by one of those catastrophes, of which even later times give us examples, broke its barrier, forcing for its waters a path to the Atlantic. May we not connect with the former existence of this inland sea the fable of the lake Parima and the El Dorado? Thousands of years may have elapsed; generations may have been buried and returned to dust; nations who once wandered on its banks may be extinct, and exist even no more in name: still the tradition of the lake Parima and the El Dorado survived these changes of time; transmitted from father to son, its fame was carried across the Atlantic, and kindled the romantic fire of the chivalric Raleigh.

Lake Amucu.

This tract contains the lake Amucu, which in the dry season is of small extent and overgrown with rushes; but during the rainy season it not only inundates the adjacent low countries, but its waters, as I have been assured by the Indians, run partly eastward into the Rupununi, and partly westward into the Rio Branco. The small river Pirara has its sources somewhat south of lake Amucu, flowing through it towards the Rio Mahu. On

Pirara.

---

* They occupy about 14,400 square miles.

the banks of this small lake stands the Macusi village Pirara. With the exception of these savannahs, and the swamps of the river Berbice, the interior is thickly wooded, the forests consisting mostly of useful timber trees.

The large rivers with which the colony is intersected continually bring down quantities of detritus. The land at the mouths of these æstuaries is therefore on the increase, forming a fringe of low ground, which is soon covered with Mangroves (*Rhizophora Mangle*) and Courida Bushes (*Avicennia nitida*); it is the first step of the shore's encroachment upon the sea. The sandy flat extends from twelve to fifteen miles to seaward, and in proportion as its distance from shore increases, it is covered with from three to four feet of water. These outskirts of new land may, it is more than probable, be hereafter gained from the sea, and form a valuable addition to the productive land. It has within the recollection of many advanced considerably, though in absence of precise data the yearly progress cannot be ascertained.

Geology.

The geology of British Guiana presents phænomena that are in accordance with what has been observed in the eastern hemisphere; the alluvial soil and clays, of which the strata along the sea-coast consists, rest upon granite; and it is to be observed as a remarkable feature, that masses which have been discovered by boring for water, at a depth of 100 feet on the coast, are to be seen at a distance of 150 miles *in situ*.

The alluvial flats are in many instances covered with a black vegetable matter, the detritus of the numerous rivers of Guiana, committed during the periodical rains to their current, and swept towards their æstuaries, where the tides have caused it to be deposited. The atmospheric air has assisted in its decomposition, and it forms now a carbonaceous vegetable matter, vulgarly called *pegass*. On the Arabisi coast of the river Essequibo, and in the vicinity of the Pomeroon, it is often found to have a depth of five to six feet.

At Ampa in the river Essequibo, a distance of about fifty miles from George Town, is an extensive bed of granite with hornblende; it has a south-western direction, appearing again at the site of the old post, in the river Mazaruni. This granitic bed has become of advantage to George Town, where it is much used for building material. A dyke, consisting of greenstone, traverses the Essequibo, and forms the first cataract in 6° 11′ N. lat.; it is called Aritaka. The rocky regions commence now, denoting primitive formation in all its component parts: granite, porphyry, and other of the extensive family of trappean rocks, may be traced at the base and on the top of the mountains. A peculiar feature are large tracts of boulders, mostly of granite, which are more or less accumulated in particular places, sometimes with great confusion; and which, wherever they traverse the rivers, form rapids and cataracts. They assume their grandest feature in that tract which is called Achra Moucra in the river Essequibo, in lat. 4° 20′. Veins of quartz frequently traverse the great masses of granite; and vast tracts of brown iron ore are met with in the mountains and the flats which extend between the rivers, from the admixture of which the soil receives a reddish tinge. This is chiefly the case in the savannahs on the Rupununi, which are frequently covered with black shining pebbles. In the vicinity of Roraima rock-crystals are found in the form of hexagonal columns, sometimes solitary, sometimes apparently agglutinated: they grow out of beds of sandstone, are perfectly transparent, and generally terminate in a single pyramid, with from three to six faces. The leading features of the mountainous regions are coloured ochres, indurated clays, granite-gneiss, and trappean rocks, and a total absence of limestone or its modifications.

Mr. Hillhouse, in his voyage up the Mazaruni, observed at some distance a conical peak, resembling the crater of a volcano*. Volcanoes and mineral springs.

There is a tradition that a volcano still in action exists up the river Siparuni, and it is mentioned by Hartzink that it had been discovered in 1749†. Though I attempted repeatedly to procure information on this subject, when in those regions, I did not succeed. If, therefore, an active volcano existed, it is probable that it is now extinct. The Indians of Pirara told me that there was, on the south-western angle of the Sierra Pacaraima, a mountain whence, from time to time, detonations are heard.

Earthquakes are very seldom felt in Guiana, and the shocks are but slight; if therefore the connexion between volcanoes and earthquakes be admitted, the rarity and slightness of the shocks do not point to the circumstance that volcanic phænomena find much fuel in Guiana. Major Staple, well known for his experiments, and in many instances for his great success in obtaining fresh water in George Town by boring, discovered a mineral spring on his own premises in Cumingsburgh, which is strongly impregnated with iron. I have frequently met with springs in the interior which were more or less impregnated with that metal, sometimes so strongly that the water was of an ochreous colour, but none which possessed thermal waters.

Guiana is not devoid of phænomena which are of interest to the geologist, and which add to the picturesque and magnificent scenery of that colony. The greatest Geological phænomena. Ataraipu, the natural pyramid.

---

* Journal of the Royal Geographical Society, vol. iv. p. 32.
† Hartzink Beschryving van Guiana, vol. i. p. 266.

geological wonder of Guiana is no doubt Ataraipu, which, with full right, may be called a natural pyramid, far surpassing in height and grandeur the Egyptian piles constructed by the labour of man.

The Ataraipu is on the western bank of the river Guidaru in 2° 55′ N. lat. Its base is wooded for about 350 feet; from thence rises the mass of granite, devoid of all vegetation, in a pyramidical form for about 550 feet more; making its whole height about 900 feet above the river.

Pouraepiapa. A column fashioned by nature, and compared by the Indians to the trunk of a crownless tree, is called Pouraepiapa, or "the felled tree," and is of great interest. It occupies the summit of a small hillock at the outskirts of the Pacaraima mountains, and is about twenty-five miles N.N.W. from the Macusi village of Pirara. This column, the regular form of which would cause any one who viewed it at some distance to suppose it to be the trunk of a decayed tree, is about fifty feet high.

Comuti or Taquiare. Two gigantic piles of granite rise on the western banks of the Essequibo, from the declivity of a hill to a height of about 140 to 150 feet. The Comuti or Taquiare consists of a huge boulder of granite, surpassing in size the celebrated pedestal of the statue of Peter I.; on this rests an oval piece of granite, which bears a third in the shape of a jar; it is covered by a fourth, and the resemblance of the two latter to a water-jar with its cover is so great, that the Indians have called it Comuti or Taquiare, which in the language of the Arawaaks and Caribs signifies respectively a jar.

Kamai. The second pile is called Kamai, which signifies the tube or strainer which is used for expressing the juice of the cassada root, before it is made into bread.

Roraima. The mural precipices of Roraima, which I have already mentioned, deserve the notice of every geologist and lover of the picturesque. They are not only remarkable for their structure, but from the cascades—the highest known, viz. 1400 to 1500 feet—which descend from them.

There are many more remarkable structures which deserved notice, if the limits of this work permitted their description;—the tracts of huge granite boulders; mountains several thousand feet high, consisting of solid granite, covered scarcely with any vegetation; the great cataracts of the rivers Corentyn, Berbice, Essequibo, which, although they offer impediments to navigation, we cannot help admiring as lovers of the picturesque.

Rivers.

The great rivers or outlets of British Guiana which drain the colony between the 57th and 60th meridian, and from the 7th parallel to the equator, are, commencing from the westward, the Essequibo, the Demerara, the Berbice, and the Corentyn.

The ESSEQUIBO* is the largest river of Guiana, and Essequibo. receives its origin in the Acarai mountains, forty-one miles north of the equator, from whence, for the first sixty miles, its general course is north-east, meandering in short turns through a rich mountain valley; it divides frequently into branches, and numerous rivulets flow from the mountains into its bed. During inundations its waters rise here from twenty-five to thirty feet above its banks. It receives the Caneruau and Wapuau from the south-east, the Camoa or Ouangou from the south-west. Having passed the Ouangou mountains, which rise on its eastern shore to a height of 3000 feet, and form the northern angle of the Acarai mountains, its

* The Essequibo is said to have received its name from Don Juan Essequibel, an officer under Diego Columbus. At its lower course it was called by the Indians who inhabited the coast 'Aranauma.' The Tarumas call the upper Essequibo 'Coatyang Kityou,' the Macusis and Caribees 'Sipou.'

course is north to the confluence of the Cassi Kityou or Yuawauri, which joins the Essequibo from the south-west. The sources of the Cassi Kityou are said to be in the vicinity of those of the Uanahau, a tributary of the Rio Branco. From this point it runs in a north-east direction, and receives in 2° 16′ N. lat. its largest tributary south of the Rupununi, the Cuyuvini, which has its sources at no great distance from those of the Rupununi, but on the eastern foot of the Carawaimi chain. The Essequibo follows now a north-western course, and is for the next seventy miles so much impeded by cataracts, that it is even not navigable for the small canoes of the natives. It forms in 3° 15′ N. lat. a large cataract called William the Fourth's Cataract. The river is here narrowed in by mountains to about fifty yards, and precipitates itself with great force over two ledges of rock about twenty-four feet high; and adopting a north-by-west direction, it receives

Rupununi. in 4° N. lat. the Rupununi, a large river which has its sources in a savannah at the western foot of the Carawaimi mountains. It forms in 2° 39′ a cataract; and meandering through the savannahs it passes the Saeraeri mountains, and flows northward through the Cannucu, until the Sierra Pacaraima, in the vicinity of the mountain Annai, turns it to the east. It receives previously, in 3° 37′ N. lat., the stream Awaricuru or Waaecuru from the south-west; by which, and its tributary the Quattata, the Pirara may be reached, which latter river belongs to the basin of the Amazon. Having passed the southern foot of the mountain Makarapan, the Rupununi receives from the south its largest tributary, the Roiwa or Rewa, and joins in lat. 3° 59′ N. the Essequibo. The course of the Rupununi is about 220 miles; it flows mostly through savannahs, and its waters are white. After its junction with the Essequibo, the latter continues in a north-western direction, forming the cataract Orotoko, and receives in lat. 4° 46' N. the River Siparuni or Red River from the south-west. In its further course the Camuti and Twasinki mountains cause it to describe almost the figure S, and it is impeded by several rapids and numerous islands. The river Potaro or Black River joins the Essequibo, from the south-west, a few miles below the cataract of Waraputa. By the Potaro and a short land-passage the Indians reach the river Mazaruni. From the hills Oumai to Point Saccaro it turns now for sixty miles due-north; while its tributary, the Mazaruni, twelve miles to the westward, and the river Demerara fifteen miles to the eastward, hold a parallel course for the same distance. Fifty miles from its mouth occur the last rapids, which prevent the tide and sailing vessels from ascending any further. About six miles north-west from Saccaro it receives the waters of the united rivers Mazaruni and Cuyuni, which at the point of junction are about a mile wide.

Mazaruni and Cuyuni.

The junction of the Mazaruni and Cuyuni takes place eight miles west of their confluence with the Essequibo. Opposite their confluence, but in the Mazaruni, is the small island Kyk-oér-all, where the Dutch in former times erected a fort against the incursions of the Spaniards. The Mazaruni is only navigable for small sailing vessels to the island of Caria; further south commence the rapids, which are no doubt caused by the same ledge of rocks that form the Aritaka rapids in the Essequibo*. The Cuyuni runs from its confluence with the Yuruario east and west. The Essequibo continues

---

* Mr. Hillhouse, who has ascended the Mazaruni and the Cuyuni to a considerable distance, found both rivers much impeded by rapids and cataracts. I suppose the Mazaruni has its sources in about 5° N. lat.; the course of the rivers Mahu, and Siparuni, and the situation of Roraima, cause me to form such an opinion.

its northern course, growing continually wider until at its mouth it forms an æstuary nearly twenty miles wide (according to others only fifteen). In its wide æstuary there are numerous islands, some of which are of considerable extent. The cultivation of Hog Island, which is about fifteen miles long, is restricted to its northern point. Wakenaam, of equal length, and Leguan, about twelve miles long, are however in a high state of cultivation. Tiger Island, the most western in the mouth of the Essequibo, is less cultivated.

The entrance of the Essequibo is much impeded and rendered dangerous for navigators by many shoals and sand-banks which extend to seaward. The best and safest of the four channels formed by the three islands is between the east shore and the Island Leguan, which has a depth of from two to four fathoms. According to the volume of water which there is in the river, the current is more or less strong; but it is seldom more than four knots, even during the rainy season. The course of the Essequibo, taking its windings into account, is not less than 620 miles, exceeding in length any river in France, and vying with the Vistula in Poland.

Demerara river. East of the Essequibo and parallel to it is the DEMERARA or DEMERARY, having its sources probably in that small group of mountains which approach the Essequibo in 4° 28′ N. lat. and are called Maccari. Its upper course is only known to the Indians. At 5° 19′ N. lat. it forms a great cataract, impassable even for canoes, which the Indians convey here overland until the river is again unimpeded. The last rapids (Kaicoutshi Rapids) are a distance of about eighty-five miles in a straight line from Georgetown, to which point it is navigable for vessels of smaller size. A square-rigged vessel has been known to load timber at Lucky Spot (in 5° 57′ N. lat.), about seventy-five miles, (the windings included,) from the river's mouth. Towards its mouth it widens to a mile, and where it enters the sea it is more than a mile and half across. A bar of mud extends about four miles to seaward, with only nine feet of water at half-flood, but the channel along the eastern shore has nineteen feet of water at high-tide. The river's average current is about $2\frac{1}{2}$ knots; it sweeps, however, with much more strength at the anchorage at Georgetown, where, assisted by the reflux of the tide, it has been known to reach a velocity of seven knots in an hour, or 11·9 feet in a second. The Demerara, running parallel between the Essequibo to the west and the Berbice to the east, does not receive any tributaries of magnitude; the tide extends about seventy-five miles in a straight line from its mouth.

The river BERBICE discharges itself into the Atlantic about fifty-seven miles to the east of the Demerara; its source is probably near the third parallel of latitude. In its upper course it approaches so near to the Essequibo that the direct distance in 3° 55′ N. lat. amounts only to nine miles. It takes from hence a north-western course, sometimes narrowing to thirty feet, at other times spreading into lake-like expansions; its banks are low and frequently marshy. The river is studded with boulders.

Berbice river.

In lat. 4° 19′ N. and about seven miles further north commence the cataracts and rapids, which impede the river for upwards of fifty miles; the last cataract is in 4° 50′ N. lat., and the river is now free for boat navigation. Where the fifth parallel crosses its course it follows a north-eastern direction to its outflow into the Atlantic. It is navigable for vessels which draw not more than twelve feet water to lat. 5° 20′, upwards of 105 miles, according to the river's winding course; vessels of seven feet draught may ascend it for 165 miles, measured along its numerous windings. The influence of the tide is perceptible nearly to that distance.

Corentyn. The river CORENTYN, or COURANTIN, forms the boundary between the Dutch and British possessions, and has its source in the same mountain-chain as the Essequibo; probably in 1° N. lat. and about twenty-five miles east of the source of the Essequibo. The river, finding its course impeded by the same tract of boulders which cut the rivers Essequibo and Berbice, expands and forms in 4° 20' a series of formidable cataracts, which in grandeur and picturesque scenery surpass any other in British Guiana. The river runs from hence north and north-east until it reaches 5° N. lat. where for about forty miles it turns west, receiving the river Cabalaba from the south; it is navigable to this point for boats that draw not more than seven feet water, a distance of about 150 miles from the sea, measured along its windings. It turns now northwards, and is so tortuous that in one instance,—namely from the mouth of the river Paruru to the river Maipuri—it describes almost a circle, the distance agreeably to the course of the river being twenty miles, while across the Savannah it is only $1\frac{3}{4}$ miles. It enters at Oreala, forty-five miles in a direct line from the embouchure, in the low plain. At Baboon Island it turns for fifteen miles north-west, assuming afterwards an almost due-northern course to its embouchure, during which distance it has a breadth of four miles. It forms in 5° 55' N. lat. an æstuary impeded by sand and mud banks, with navigable channels between. The breadth of this æstuary between the Plantation Mary's Hope and Nickeri, which is considered the mouth of the Corentyn, is in a north-west and south-east line ten miles; others consider Gordon's Point and the Plantation Alness as the extreme points of the mouth of the Corentyn; which would give a breadth of upwards of eighteen geographical miles across. The windward channel is the deepest for entering the Corentyn; it has 8½ feet water at low water, and the tide rises 8½ feet at springs, and 3 feet at neap. On the western shore is a sand-bank with 7 feet water at low tide.

The Corentyn, before entering the sea, receives on its eastern shore the river Nickeri: at its mouth and on its right bank is the Dutch Settlement Nickeri, with a battery and garrison of 120 men, regular troops.

Between the Essequibo and Orinoco are the rivers Pomeroon, Marocco, and Wai-ina or Guayma; and although these outlets are comparatively of small size, they are so closely connected by branches and tributaries, that they afford an inland navigation from the Marocco to the Orinoco. Their importance in a political and commercial respect becomes therefore evident. Pomeroon, Marocco, and Guayma.

Between the Demerara and the Berbice are the small rivers Mahaica, Mahaiconi, and Abari. Mahaica, Mahaiconi, Abari.

Between the Berbice and Corentyn there is at present no outlet: the "Devil's Creek," which the Dutch claim as their boundary, is completely choked up by sand, and was when in existence merely the outlet of the swampy ground behind the sea-coast in that region.

Climate.

Though Guiana is situated in the torrid zone, it enjoys comparatively a more temperate climate than other countries under the same latitude. The mean temperature for the year is 81°·2, the maximum 90°, the minimum 74°. It is generally considered that two wet and two dry seasons constitute the changes during the year. However regular the setting-in of these periods may have been formerly, this has not been the case during General description of the annual changes.

later years*. The great dry season commences at the coast regions towards the end of August, and continues to the end of November, after which showers of rain follow to the end of January: the short dry season commences in the middle of February, and continues to the middle of April. The rains descend afterwards in torrents, and the rivers commence to inundate their shores. During that period the wind is frequently from the west and south-west, and, coming from the land, is thought unhealthier than the regular sea-breeze, which during the dry season begins to set in between ten and eleven A.M., and continues until sunset, sometimes even through the night. The months of October and November are the most delightful in the year; the sky cloudless, the heat moderate, and the thermometer at noontide scarcely higher than 85° Fahr. During the rainy season the oppressive weight of the atmosphere is tempered by northern breezes, and in the months of September to November the breezes from the east and south-east, which have passed over a vast extent of the ocean, are invigorating, and refresh the air to such a degree, that during the night the thermometer has been known to fall to 74° Fahr.

The moisture necessary to maintain vegetation is then replaced by dew; and not only in the interior, where the country is not extensively cleared, but likewise in the open savannahs, the trees and plants will be found in the morning dripping with dew.

* The change is equally uncertain in the interior, and the expedition which I had the honour to command was six weeks longer delayed in the interior in 1839, there not being sufficient water in the rivers to navigate them. The Rio Negro, whose rise is generally considered to commence in the beginning of March, did not rise until April, and at the large savannahs the rain only set in that year in May.

The change of the seasons is marked by severe thunder-storms; but however loud the peals of thunder may reverberate, and however vivid the flashes of lightning which precede them, fatal accidents by lightning are unknown in Guiana. Gales are scarcely known, much less those terrific phænomena of nature hurricanes, which in the neighbouring islands destroy in a brief time the fruits of many years' labour, causing devastation and loss of life to a vast extent.

A few shocks of earthquake are occasionally felt, but they are so insignificant that the inhabitants scarcely notice them when they occur.

The temperature of the interior is still more mild, and the climate healthy. The season in the interior is only marked by two changes; from the month of August to the month of March there are only occasional showers, but from March to August the rain descends in torrents, and the rivers commence to swell and overflow their banks, to a greater or less extent according to their locality.

The following meteorological register was noted in Georgetown, and has been politely communicated to me.

Meteorological Tables kept in Georgetown and in the interior.

Month.	BAROMETER, in English inches and decimals.				THERMOMETER. Fahrenheit.			
	Highest.	Lowest.	Mean.	Greatest Range.	Highest.	Lowest.	Mean.	Greatest Range.
January...	29·99	29·84	29·912	·15	85	75	80·225	10°
February..	29·97	29·83	29·890	·14	86	75	79·69	11
March.....	30·05	29·86	29·959	·19	85	75	80·35	10
April	30·00	29·84	29·911	·16	86	78	81·7	8
May	30·02	29·85	29·927	·17	86	75	81·10	11
June	30·02	29·86	29·942	·16	86	76	81·166	10
July	30·00	29·85	29·938	.15	86	76	80·964	10
August	30·04	29·83	29·949	·21	89	78	82·532	11
September	30·00	29·74	29·878	·26	88	79	83·316	9
October ...	29·99	29·80	29·904	·19	89	78	83·5	11
November.	29·96	29·77	29·883	·19	90	77	82·366	12
December.	30·01	29·82	29·905	·19	87	75	80·19	12

The annual result is therefore as follows:

BAROMETER.				THERMOMETER.			
Highest.	Lowest.	Mean.	Greatest Range.	Highest.	Lowest.	Mean.	Greatest Range.
30·05	29·74	29·916	31	90°	75°	81·226°	15°

By a daily register of the temperature of the air in the shade between 6ʰ A.M. and 6ʰ P.M., and between the parallels of 2° 36′ and 6° 49′ N. lat. I received from October 1835 to March 31st 1836 the following data:

FAHRENHEIT'S SCALE.							
	Oct.	Nov.	Dec.	Jan.	Feb.	Mar.	Total.
Highest	87·5°	89°	86·5°	88·9°	85·9°	84°	°
Mean	79·1	82	80·1	82	81	76·5	
Lowest	68	72	68·5	75	74	69	
Number of rainy days with little intermission	*12	2	11	6	12	27	70
Days with little rain	9	10	11	16	12	4	62
Fair without rain	10	18	9	9	5	0	51

The mean of observations at 6ʰ and 9ʰ A.M., 12ʰ, 3ʰ and 6ʰ P.M., in 1838, during a stay of three months in Pirara, situated in the middle of the savannahs on the banks of the lake Amucu, in lat. 3° 39′ N., long. 59° 16′ W., and 600 feet above the level of the sea, give the following results:

Month.	BAROMETER, in English inches and decimal parts.				THERMOMETER. Fahrenheit's scale.			
	Highest.	Lowest.	Mean.	Greatest Range.	Highest.	Lowest.	Mean.	Greatest Range.
April	29·500″	29·286″	29·394″	·214	93·5°	73°	82·3°	20·5°
May	29·500	29·292	29·410	·208	91	73·5	81	17·5
June	29·496	29·310	29·429	·186	90	73·5	81·07	16·5

* It will be necessary to remark that the years 1835 and 1836 were considered to be more rainy than usual; this observation refers likewise to the coast-regions.

These observations were continued during the months of July and August at Fort Saõ Joaquim do Rio Branco, in lat. 3° 1′ N. and long. 60° 3′ W., and gave the following results:

Month.	BAROMETER, in English inches and decimal parts.				THERMOMETER. Fahrenheit's scale.			
	Highest.	Lowest.	Mean.	Greatest Range.	Highest.	Lowest.	Mean.	Greatest Range.
July	29·722	29·500	29·6211	·222	86°·5	74°·8	80·69	11°·7
August......	29·730	29·500	29·6178	·230	88	76	82·16	12

The night is generally from 8° to 10° cooler than the day. A greater difference prevails however at the table-land, from which Roraima rises to a height of 7000 feet; there I have known a difference of 35° in the range of the thermometer, compared at the hours of five in the morning and two in the afternoon. At this table-land, which was only elevated about 3000 feet above the sea, the thermometer half an hour before sunrise ranged between 59° and 62°, and rose between two and three o'clock in the afternoon to 95° in the shade.

When the heat of the air is greatest, the temperature of the water in the rivers is at its lowest comparative point; and during night, but chiefly towards sunrise, the water is about 10° warmer than the air. The Indian takes his customary bath generally in the morning, when the water is most congenial to the feelings. A number of experiments have shown me that

_{Temperature of the running waters.}

at 6ʰ A.M. the water is generally from 8° to 10° warmer than the air.
at 2ʰ P.M. the air is generally from 1° to 2° warmer than the water.
at 6ʰ P.M. the water is generally from 2° to 3° warmer than the air.

The climate of British Guiana has been described as unhealthy, and detrimental to European settlers; consequently emigrants have rather preferred encountering

_{Influence of the climate on the health of the inhabitants.}

the chilly blasts and severe winters of Canada and the United States, or to subject themselves to the horrors of a prolonged voyage to Australia, there to suffer expatriation perhaps for ever from their native homes and families, than to settle in a colony where constant summer prevails, and which, with the nigh establishment of regular steam-boats to those parts, may be reached in sixteen or seventeen days from England.

But by a comparison of facts, it may be demonstrated that the climate of British Guiana ensures as great a duration of life as that of many European countries. It has been proved " that the range of mortality even among the labouring population, is about one in thirty-seven to forty, but in London and France it is equal as regards the whole population, rich and poor, and in other countries it is even more: thus in Naples one in thirty-four; Wirtemberg, one in thirty-three; Paris, one in thirty-two; Madrid, one in twenty-nine; Rome, one in twenty-five; Amsterdam, one in twenty-four; Vienna, one in twenty-two and a half: and a comparison of the mortality in Demerara and the healthy county of Rutlandshire in England, proves that duration of life is in favour of the colony *."

The fatal cholera which committed such destruction in Asia, Europe, and America, and which in Quebec carried to the grave a tenth of its whole population, was never felt in Guiana, neither was the influenza or the grippe.

The endemic disease in 1837 to 1839.

When physicians were unacquainted with the proper method of treating the yellow fever, many Europeans fell victims to that disease. Medical men are at present more successful in its treatment, and for many years it had totally disappeared. After an interval of fifteen years it showed itself again in 1837, and was evidently to be

* Montgomery Martin's History of the West Indies, vol. ii. p. 33–34.

ascribed to local causes, namely to the neglected state of the sewers and the filth accumulated between the wharfs. The wharfs, which extend along Water-street or the commercial part of Georgetown, were formerly erected upon piles, and the tide had full access to carry off whatever filth had accumulated: at a later period these wharfs have been erected of masonwork, and as a separate wharf is generally attached to every lot or building, openings have remained between them which are too narrow to allow the tide to enter freely and to sweep away the impure matter thrown there by neglect. The rapid decomposition of animal and vegetable matter under the tropics created in this instance an effluvium, which is generally considered by the physicians in the colony to have been the cause of the late calamity. It showed itself therefore first in Water-street, and was mostly restricted to that quarter of the town: it spread next among the shipping which were anchored in front of these wharfs, where it prevailed with great mortality among the sailors. In the infected part of the town a faint and sickly smell was perceived; and it has been, I believe, generally acknowledged and proved, that those who were attacked by the disease out of town or in Berbice, had previously visited Water-street and breathed the noxious exhalations. Immediate contact with the sick did not propagate the disease, nor did seclusion diminish it; and there is no instance known in which it extended to the more elevated places in the interior.

The general health of the town was restored in 1839, when on a sudden the distemper made its appearance among the garrison at the barracks, somewhat east of the town, where it committed frightful ravages among the European troops. The beach to the eastward of these barracks is covered with mangroves and *Curida* bushes, and the muddy ground beneath them diffuses noxious exhalations, which are materially increased by the decomposition of numerous mollusca, insects, and crustaceous animals, which seek shelter from the waves among the interlaced roots, and frequently perish there. The wind and tide carry the drift matter which comes down the river or from among the shipping ashore here, and it accumulates, and contributes to the insalubrity of the air. The frequently intemperate and indolent life of the soldiers assisted to increase the disease, and it did not stay its ravages until the soldiers were removed to Georgetown and to the country. The troops in Berbice and in the outposts remained healthy during this period, and it is worthy to be noted that during a space of fourteen years no officer of the line died in Berbice. There were only two deaths among commissioned officers during that period, namely a barrack-master and a surgeon.

Number of deaths in Georgetown in 1837, during the prevalence of the endemic.

I am not acquainted with the number of deaths which occurred among the garrison during the prevalence of these awful endemic attacks; but I possess the official return of the Colony sexton of the year 1837, when the unhealthiness of Georgetown and the existence of the yellow fever could not be denied. The burials amounted during that year to 914, namely,—

  428 white persons, including 97 seamen,
  160 apprenticed labourers,
  326 coloured persons.

In absence of data it is difficult, if not impossible, to form an estimate of the number of deaths in a given number of inhabitants. The population of Georgetown amounted in 1829 to 1620 whites, 4368 free coloured, and 6616 slaves. On the 31st of May 1832, we observe from official returns that the slaves in Georgetown amounted to 8033; and as in the interval no census had been taken, the actual number of inhabitants, when the yellow fever first showed itself, cannot be ascertained. The number of emigrants who arrived in 1837 amounted to 2050. The number of white inhabitants have been stated to be between 4000 to 5000 in 1837, which, deducting the 97 seamen, gives—

1 death in 15 persons among the whites and coloured,
1 —— 50 —————— apprenticed labourers,
or about five per cent. of the whole population; while previous to the endemic disease and after the present restoration of health, the number of deaths amounted scarcely to three per cent.

The following statement of the annual mortality on five estates in Berbice is taken from parliamentary papers, and will show the annual mortality among the labouring classes.

Number of apprenticed labourers in 1835, 1309; in 1836, 1271; in 1837, to 30th Nov., 1226.

Number of deaths during 1835, 38; in 1836, 38; in 1837, to 30th Nov., 31.

38 deaths in 1309 give 1 in $34\frac{2}{3}$ as the average of 1835
45 —— 1271 — 1 in $28\frac{1}{2}$ ———— 1836
34 —— 1226 — 1 in 36 ———— 1837;

—a mortality less than the average of several European nations, and very little more than that within the bills of mortality in London. The above statement proves further the salubrity of 1837 in Berbice, during which year the endemic was prevailing in Georgetown, and restricts the latter to local causes. It will be observed that the least number of deaths occurred in 1837, if compared with the preceding two years.

Let us now compare the number of deaths among the labouring classes in the West India Islands, and it will become evident that mortality is more fatal in Trinidad, Tobago, St. Vincent's, Grenada, Dominica, than in Demerara.

The number of deaths between the years 1820 and 1832 among the labouring population, when still slaves, gave the annual average in

Trinidad of	1 in 23
Tobago	1 — 24
Demerara and Essequibo	1 — 33
Berbice	1 — 32
Jamaica	1 — 40
Grenada	1 — 30
St. Vincent's	1 — 32
Barbadoes	1 — 35
St. Lucia	1 — 34
Dominica	1 — 32
Antigua	1 — 36
St. Christopher's	1 — 36
Montserrat	1 — 34
Nevis	1 — 41

Salubrity of the climate of the interior. The salubrity of the interior is proverbial, and there are many instances of longevity among the settlers on the banks of the rivers Berbice, Demerara, and Essequibo*. The natural drainage is here so perfect, that all impurities are swept off by the torrents of rain; and the purity of the air so great, that the planets Venus and Jupiter may be seen in the day-time †. The climate inland is re-

---

* Instances of longevity are not unfrequent at the coast regions. There is a monumental inscription in the parish of St. Saviour's, on the Corentyn coast, that the deceased, a Mr. Baird, after a residence of fifty-three years in the West Indies, the last thirty-six of which were spent on the Corentyn coast, had reached the advanced age of eighty-seven years and eight months. I am acquainted with several instances of Europeans now residing in Guiana, who have passed thirty to forty years in the colony without having visited Europe in the interval, and enjoy excellent health.

† While descending the Upper Essequibo in December 1838, we saw, one afternoon at three o'clock, the sun, the moon, and the planet Venus.

storative, and the writer has been assured by several individuals who reside generally in the coast regions, that when they are ailing they undertake an excursion in the interior, and are sure to return after a short period in health. It is not the absolute degree of temperature which determines the salutary state of a country, but the sudden changes of heat and cold; and, as will have been observed from the preceding tables, the uniformity of the temperature is so great in Guiana, that it is not surpassed by any country under the globe.

The climate of Guiana is free from those alternations of heat and cold, and those chilly piercing winds with a hot sun, not uncommon in some of the islands.

Tubercular consumption is unknown on the coast. Many who have arrived with this complaint from Europe or the northern part of America have perfectly recovered *; and Dr. Hancock assures us that, during his long practice on the coast of Guiana, he " never met with an instance of genuine tubercular phthisis, nor a single case of calculus generated there. Now," he continues, " this is not the case amongst the West India Islands, and for this plain reason; that however favourable may be the sea-breeze in the day, there is every night a cool land-wind blowing from the central parts towards the sea†." *Tubercular consumption unknown in Guiana. The colony a place of resort for northern invalids.*

The prevailing diseases are dysenteries, diarrhœa and fevers: the latter prevail chiefly in the intermitting form throughout the swampy land, which runs level with the sea-coast; but they may be guarded against by due at- *Indolence and intemperance the cause of the great mortality among European colonists.*

* The West Indies have lately been recommended as places of resort for northern invalids afflicted with dyspepsia, nervous complaints, and pulmonary diseases. See " A Winter in the West Indies and Florida."

† Dr. Hancock relates an instance in which the climate of Guiana proved curative of pulmonary consumption in a most remarkable and desperate case, in the person of a Swede who arrived in a vessel from Portsmouth.

tention to perspiration; indeed exercise and temperance are the greatest safeguards. The opinion that Europeans are not able to undergo exercise or labour under the tropics, is a great mistake; those who take daily exercise, without exposing themselves to the heat of the vertical sun, and abstain from the excessive use of strong liquors, may enjoy the best health and a long life. Indolence and intemperance have carried more victims to the grave than any endemic disease which ever prevailed in Guiana.

I have dwelt longer on the effects which climate exercises on the inhabitants of British Guiana than properly belongs to the plan of this little work: it became, however, necessary to prove that the colony is really not so unhealthy as public opinion holds it to be. It is to be hoped that more attention will be paid to the important work of draining and clearing unoccupied lots in the towns. If the local authorities, on whom the necessary orders for the accomplishment of this depend, reflect for a moment on the importance of impressing, with a favorable opinion of British Guiana, those countries from which the colony expects to draw emigrants, no exertion or expense ought to be spared to promote and increase the healthiness of their towns. The most injurious reports with regard to the fatal influence of the climate on European constitutions have gone forth, and have been spread through Europe; and, with the same incorrectness that Demerara has been styled an island in parliamentary speeches, it has been designated a charnel-house.

Vegetable Productions.

Few countries on the surface of the globe can be compared with Guiana for vigour and luxuriance of vegetation. A constant summer prevails; and the fertility of the soil, the humid climate, and congenial temperature, insure a succession of flowers and fruits; in a person accustomed to the sleep of nature in the northern regions, where vegetation is deprived of its greatest charms, the leafy crown and the fragrant blossoms cannot but raise astonishment and admiration.

Diversified with hills, plains, forests and meadows, a country so extensive offers various productions. These have been increased by introductions from other parts of the world, and present objects of industry and enterprize, which insure to the poor maintenance, to the labourer the liberal recompense of his toil, to the merchant commerce, and to the capitalist an increase of his wealth.

The majestic scenes of nature which I viewed during my exploring tours in Guiana impressed themselves with indelible characters upon my mind, which are the more powerfully awakened, since my return to Europe, when comparing our vegetation with the magnificent scenes which plain, dale, or forest present under the tropics.

The coasts, washed by the waves of the Atlantic Ocean, are covered with mangrove and *Curida* bushes*, and present a verdure of perpetual freshness, forming as it were a seam or fringe to the rich carpet behind. They are enlivened by numerous flocks of the scarlet Ibis, the white Egrette, and the splendid Flamingo, which, disturbed at the approach of an intruder, soar into the air, or perch on the summits of the trees. Where cultivation has not stamped its seal on the landscape, the marshy plain changes to savannah, resembling the meadows of Europe, watered by rivers and limpid streams, inter-

* The vegetation along the coast, as elsewhere alluded to, consists chiefly of *Rhizophora Mangle*, L., *Avicennia nitida* and *tomentosa*, and *Conocarpus erectus*.

spersed by groups of palms or tufts of trees. On ascending the great rivers, which have been happily called " the veins of the country," we find them covered with verdant isles; and as we approach the primitive forests the landscape assumes the features peculiar to the tropics. It appears as if the power and strength of productive nature in recoiling from the poles had collected itself near the equator, and spread its gifts with open hand, to render its aspect more imposing and majestic, and to manifest the fecundity of the soil. Gigantic trees raise their lofty crowns to a height unknown in the European forest, and display the greatest contrast in the form and appearance of their foliage*. Lianas cling to their trunks, interlace their wide-spreading branches, and, having reached their summit, their aërial roots descend again towards the ground, and appear like the cordage of a ship. Clusters of palm-trees, of all the vegetable forms the most grand and beautiful, rise majestically above the surrounding vegetation, waving their pinion-like leaves in the soft breeze. Nature, as if not satisfied with the soil allotted to her, decorates with profuse vegetation the trunks and limbs of trees, the stones and rocks; even the surface of the water is covered with a carpet of plants interspersed by magnificent flowers†. What could better give an idea of the luxuriance and richness of vegetation in Guiana, than the splendid *Victoria regia,* the most beau-

* If we except the *Coniferæ*, our forest trees, as oaks, birches, ashes, cannot vie in size with the *Laurineæ*, the Icica and Mora of the tropical forest.

† The magnificent *Victoria regia,* which the author was so fortunate as to discover on the 1st of January, 1837, in the river Berbice, and which Her Majesty has graciously consented to have made known by that name, covers, in conjunction with the azure-coloured Pontedera, divers *Utriculariæ,* a species of *Polygonum, Pistia,* and numerous *Gramineæ,* occasionally the whole surface of the river Berbice so as to impede navigation.

tiful specimen of the flora of the western hemisphere? The calm of the atmosphere, where frequently no breath of wind agitates the foliage, no cloud veils the azure vault of heaven, contrasts strongly with the hum of animated nature produced by insects of every kind. The humming bird with its metallic lustre passes rapidly from blossom to blossom, sipping the nectar of fragrant flowers, or sporting with the dewdrop which glitters on its leaf.

It is usual to deny to the birds of the American forest all melody. Many are the feathered songsters which enliven the forest: although they may not vie with our nightingale in melodiousness of tone, they are not devoid of it. Night approaches, and displays the firmament with all the splendour of the southern constellations; the musical notes of birds now give place to the chirping voices of crickets, the sounds of the tree-frog, lizards and reptiles. Thousands of phosphorescent insects flutter among the foliage, emitting a light, which, if it does not illuminate, assists to increase the characteristic features of a tropical night.

The dense and almost impenetrable forest of the interior offers inexhaustible treasures, not only for architecture in all its branches, but likewise for the manufacture of furniture, and for many other purposes that minister to the restoration of health or to the comfort and luxury of man.

Not less productive in medicinal herbs are the savannahs; and an enumeration of the various useful trees and herbs would fill sheets. I shall therefore satisfy myself with mentioning only those the use of which is fully acknowledged by the colonists and natives.

The MORA (*Mora excelsa*, Benth.) may well be called the king of the forest; it towers above every other tree, and reaches frequently a height of 120 feet. It is abundant in the interior, and its wood so close and cross-grained that it is difficult to split it. It is considered

Timber-trees.

by the most competent judges to be superior to oak, (as it is not subject to the dry-rot,) and the very best wood that can be procured for ships' timbers. It can be obtained from ten to twenty inches square, and thirty to fifty feet long; and its branches having a tendency to grow crooked, it affords natural knees, while the trunk might be used for keels, beams and planking.

SIPERI, or GREEN HEART, (belonging to the natural family of *Laurineæ*,) is one of the most useful timber-trees which Guiana possesses. It grows to a height of about sixty feet, and is often two feet in diameter; it is a fine-grained and hard wood, well adapted for the planking of vessels and for house-frames.

The seeds are of the size of a walnut, and possess a strong bitter, which has been extracted by Dr. Rodie, and been used with great advantage as a powerful febrifuge.

In times of scarcity the Indians grate the fruit and immerse it in water, by which process the fecula sinks to the bottom; the flour thus obtained is mixed with rotten wood, pounded and sifted; the bread prepared is bitter and disagreeable.

The black GREEN HEART is scarce. Its wood is in great request in the islands, as from its well-known durability it is preferred to all others for windmills, shafts, spindles, rollers, arms, water-wheel planks, &c.

The PURPLE HEART is rather scarce on the coast-regions. It is a tree of the largest size, and its wood is used for furniture in consequence of the beauty of its colour and its durability; its elasticity is very great; it has been used with advantage for the construction of mortar-beds*. The Indians call the Purple Heart *mari*

---

* Col. Moody, of the Royal Engineers, observes, that the "black Green Heart" and the "Purple Heart," were the only woods which stood the test, while all others failed, as mortar-beds at the siege of Fort Bourbon at Martinique.

wayana. They take off the bark of this tree when fresh cut down, and with very little trouble convert it into a canoe, commonly called a "wood-skin," some of which are large enough to carry twenty to twenty-five persons with perfect safety on smooth water.

KAKARALLI is very plentiful, and may be had from six to fourteen inches square, and from thirty to forty feet long. It is preferred in the colony to most timbers, and possesses the peculiarity, that the sea-worm or barnacle never attacks it.

WAMARA may be had from six to twelve inches square, and twenty to forty feet long. It is hard and cross-grained, consequently not apt to split; it would therefore answer various purposes in naval architecture.

DETERMA is very plentiful, squaring from six to twenty inches, and may be had from thirty to sixty feet long. It is much used in the colony for the construction of schooners; it ought to be copper-fastened, as iron nails are apt to corrode.

HOUBABALLI is very close and fine-grained, and much used in the colony for furniture. It takes a beautiful polish. It may be had from six to fifteen inches square, and from twenty to thirty-five feet long.

WALLABA is very abundant throughout the colony. It is a reddish-brown wood, and splits smoothly and freely; it is used for staves, shingles, &c. The wood possesses an oily resin, the use of which is however not known.

BULLY-TREE is a tree of the first size; it is often six feet in diameter. The weather appears to have little influence upon it, and it is therefore preferred for house-frames, posts, floors, &c. The branches are cut into shingles for covering houses; it squares from twenty to thirty inches, and may be had thirty to sixty feet long.

SIRUABALLI (a *Laurus*) is much used for planking, and has been found to resist the attack of worms, in consequence of a bitter principle which it contains. It is light, and floats; boat-builders use it for the construction of gigs, boats, &c.

CUAMARA, or Tonkin Bean, is not only valuable for its seeds, but it is likewise a useful timber-tree. Its wood is very hard, and it has been ascertained that a timber one inch square and of a given length bears one hundred pounds more weight than any other timber in Guiana of the same dimensions: it is therefore fit for anything where great pressure is the object.

CABACALLI may be had from twelve to twenty inches square, and thirty to fifty feet long. It is durable and very hard, and is used for beams and posts.

CARANA, WAHLI, or Cedar-wood, abounds in the interior of Guiana, and is much esteemed in consequence of its durability. It possesses a resin, which is odorous. The tree reaches a height of sixty to eighty feet, and is highly recommended for the construction of masts, spars, &c. The bark is red and astringent.

HUCOUYA, or Iron-wood, grows to the height of fifty feet, and is often six feet in diameter. It has a reddish wood, which becomes dark by age. It is uncommonly hard, as the name denotes, but not very durable when exposed to wet. It is used for fitting out the interior of houses.

SI-TO-OH-BALLI, or BOURRA-COURRA, or LETTER-WOOD, is one of the costliest woods which Guiana possesses. It is of a beautiful brown colour, with black spots, which have been compared to hieroglyphics; the spotted part being only peculiar to the heart, which is seldom more than twelve to fifteen inches in circumference: it is only adapted for work of small size, and for veneering; but its beauty is so great that it surpasses every other wood for elegant appearance.

SIMIRI, or LOCUST TREE, reaches often a height of from sixty to eighty feet, and seven to eight feet in diameter. The wood is hard and compact, and is of a fine brown colour streaked with veins; it takes a beautiful polish, and is consequently much used for furniture. Its durability recommends it for the use of mill-rollers; it yields abundantly a kind of resin (gum-animé), much resembling gum-copal.

The BISI is a gigantic tree, and its wood is of great durability; the Indians use it for constructing corials and canoes; it yields a resin of a greenish colour, which is used by the Indians to give a gloss to their bows, &c.

DUCALI-BALLI, ITIKIRIBOURRA-BALLI, BANNIA are recommended for ornamental work. The Itikiribourra-balli is of a rich brown, spotted like a tiger-skin, in consequence of which it is called in the colony tiger-wood; as in the Letter-wood it is only the heart of the tree which can be used.

The YARI-YARI, or Lance-wood, is a slender tree, and possesses much toughness and elasticity. The natives make their arrow-points of it, and in the colony it is used for shafts of carriages, and large quantities of the spars are exported to Europe.

YARURI, MASSARA, or Paddle-wood. The whole tree, five to six feet in diameter, and to the first branches perhaps fifty feet high, has the appearance of being fluted, or as if it consisted of numerous slender trees. The flat or tabular projections of the lower part of the trunk are used by the natives for the construction of their paddles. The wood is light, elastic, and very strong; it might prove advantageous for gun-carriages, bulwarks of vessels of war, &c., as, besides its elasticity it is not apt to splinter.

The wood of the SOUARI greatly resembles in nature and properties that of the Mora, and may be obtained from twenty to forty feet long, and sixteen to twenty inches square.

The SIRUBA, a tree of the first size, is only found in the interior, and is much used in the colony for ship-building. It yields by incision a camphoraceous fluid.

The ANAPAIMA abounds in the rocky district; it is a tree of the first size, and its wood is close-grained. The bark is highly aromatic, and is used by the Indians in fevers and dysentery.

CRAB WOOD grows tall and straight, and is used for masts and spars in colony vessels. It is a light and red wood and employed for floors and partitions in house-building.

TATABA grows tall and to a large size. It is a hard and tough wood, well adapted for mill timbers and planks of all descriptions, also for ship-building, gun-carriages, coffee-stamps, &c.

TACCUBA. This wood very much resembles the WASHIBA, or Bow-wood, and is only to be found in the high lands and among the falls. It is strong, hard, and durable, but not so elastic as the Washiba.

This list of timber-trees exhibits only such as are most advantageously known in the colony; but there are numerous others equally useful, although not yet generally known to the colonist*.

In medicinal respects many vegetable productions are of acknowledged value, but I shall refer to them under

* The information regarding the use of native timber-trees has been politely communicated to me by Mr. Patterson, an experienced ship-wright and wood-cutter.

another article when I allude to the capabilities and resources of the Colony.

Animal Kingdom.

The Western Hemisphere does not equal in number nor in size the quadrupeds of Asia and Africa. The Jaguar, or South American Tiger, the Puma or American Lion, and several others of the Cat species, are the most ferocious; nevertheless, there are but few instances known where they have attacked man; and they are only feared as depredators on the flocks of cattle and sheep of the colonists. *(Quadrupeds.)*

It is not my intention to enter in this work, the extent of which is limited, into a description of the animals which are indigenous to Guiana: I shall content myself with enumerating such as contribute to the wants of man, affording a wholesome and delicate food. To this belong the Tapir or Maipuri, the Capibara or Waterhaas, the Labba, the Aguti, the Acuchi, the Cairuni or Wild-hog, the Peccari or Mexican Hog, and Deer of different species; other animals are the Ant-eater, Armadillo, Sloth, Otters, several species of Polecats, and Opossums. Numerous herds and varieties of Monkeys people the otherwise solitary forest, and serve as food to the natives. The Manati, Lamantine, or Sea-cow, is from time to time met with in the larger rivers: its flesh is white and delicate, and has been compared in taste to veal.

Not less numerous are the Birds; and while some astonish us by their magnificent plumage, others fully make up for their deficiency in this respect by their delicate and nutritious flesh. To the latter belong divers species of Wild Ducks, the Powis, the Marudi, the Hannaqua resembling a pheasant, the Duraqua and Maam, both resembling the European Partridge, Wild Pigeons, &c. *(Birds.)*

Among divers others I have yet to mention the Jabiru or Tararamu, a large bird which frequents the savannahs, and the flesh of which is not unlike beef in taste,—Parrots, Macaws, the plumage of which glows with the most vivid tints of blue, purple and yellow; the numerous species of Humming-birds covered with the most gorgeous plumage, and glittering with metallic lustre when winging their way from flower to flower; the Toucan, the bright yellow and black Mocking-birds, which construct their pendent nests on the same branch with the wild bees or the wasps, with which it appears they have entered into alliance, and receive their protection. The most courageous of the monkeys or the wariest of the cats would not attempt a depredation on their eggs as long as under the respected protection of these insects. The Bell-bird or Campanero, white as snow, with a leathery excrescence on its head, the cry of which has been resembled to the tolling of a convent bell; the magnificent Cock-of-the-rock with its bright orange plumage, and its head surmounted by a semi-circular erect crest, convey an idea of the splendour with which nature has decked its offspring under the tropics.

Saurians. Of the Saurian tribe the Caiman and Alligator are perhaps the most formidable. The latter is too small to become dangerous; frequently, however, as I have met with the former, I never observed any disposition in them to attack us, unless we had provoked them. The Alligator inhabits the coast regions; the Caiman is only found in the interior. The Guana, which has the appearance of an overgrown lizard, is from four to six feet long, including the tail: it is entirely harmless, and its flesh is declared very delicate by every one who has overcome the prejudice which its appearance generally creates.

Turtles. Land Tortoises and fresh-water Turtles are very abundant, the latter chiefly in the river Essequibo and its tributaries. They assemble in large numbers during the time that the female deposits her eggs on the sandy shore or banks of the rivers. The eggs are very delicate, and are eaten fresh and smoked by the Indians; or they prepare a sweet-tasted oil of it, which is much used for culinary purposes by the Brazilians*.

Several of the Serpents of Guiana are poisonous; but as if in some measure to guard against their formidable quality, nature has rendered them less dangerous by making them sluggish and loath to bite, unless irritated. The Conocushi or Bush-master, the Rattle-snake, the Labaria, the Parrot and Guana Snake, the Capairu and Scarlet Snake are among the most dangerous. The Camudi and Colukunaru belong to the genus *Boa*; but the instances where they are known to have attacked man are very few; they satisfy themselves with surprising deer and other smaller animals. [Serpents.]

The rivers of the interior teem with delicious Fish in great variety. The Arapaima or Pirarucu (*Sudis Gigas*), and a species of *Silurus*, the Lau-lau, are from ten to twelve feet long, and weigh from two to three hundred pounds. The Luganani or Sun-fish, the Haimura, Bashaw, Cartabac, Killbagre, the delicious Pacu, the Arouan, the Paiara, Pirai, the Morocoto or Osibu, the Laukidi, the Parrau, &c. vie in delicacy with any of our European freshwater fishes, while numerous others contribute equally to the nutriment of man. [Fish.]

Among Insects, some species of ants prove destructive to vegetation; and the *Termites*, or White Ants, are known [Insects.]

---

* The turtle oil (*mantega de tartaruga*) constitutes a branch of commerce in the province of Para. The quantity which is prepared only in the Upper Amazons, or Solimoes, is estimated at eight thousand potes of two arrobas or sixty-four pounds each.

to have become injurious to the framework of houses, or to furniture, if they are allowed to take up their residence in a dwelling. The sting of the Scorpion and the bite of the Centipede are painful, but not dangerous. It is chiefly confined to old rubbish and houses. The bite of the Bush-spider, and what is here called the Tarantula, produces inflammation of the part where the bite has been inflicted, but has never endangered life. The Tshiko or Chigo, a small species of flea which penetrates into the skin of the feet, proves frequently very troublesome; it infests abandoned huts, chiefly where there is a sandy soil; cleanliness in great measure banishes it.

Musquitoes are not frequent in the interior; but some regions are infested by a small fly called Mapire (*Simulia*), which proves troublesome by its bites.

STATISTICS OF BRITISH GUIANA.

British Guiana consists of the counties of Demerara, Essequibo, and Berbice. Demerara and Essequibo have been united, and are divided into the following eleven parishes.

Political Division.

1. ST. MARY, extending from the Abari Creek to plantation Lowlands.
2. ST. PAUL, from plantation Nooten's Zuile to plantation Cuming's Lodge.
3. ST. GEORGE AND ST. ANDREW, comprehending Georgetown, and extending from thence to plantation Turkeyen.
4. ST. MATTHEW, plantation Penitence and east bank of river Demerara.
5. ST. MARK, plantation Mindenberg Canal, No. 1, and west bank of Demerara river upwards.
6. ST. SWITHIN, from plantation La Grange to plantation La Jalousie.
7. ST. LUKE, plantation Blankenburg up east bank of river Essequibo.
8. ST. PETER, Leguan and Hog Islands.
9. ST. JAMES, Wakenaam and Trooli islands.
10. ST. JOHN, from Schoonhooven to Capooey Creek.
11. TRINITY, from Capooey Creek to Pomeroon river.

The county of Berbice is divided into six parishes.

1. ALL SAINTS, comprehending the town New Amsterdam, plantations Overwinning and Providence, and the left bank of the river Canje.
2. ST. PATRICK, right bank of the river Canje and the east coast canal.
3. ST. MICHAEL, from plantation Balthyock to the river Abari.
4. ST. CATHERINE, from plantations Zorg and Hoop to plantation Herstelling, and the west bank of the Berbice river.
5. ST. CLEMENT, from plantation Everton to plantation Onderneeming, east bank of river Berbice.

6. St. Saviour, the Corentyn coast and river.

The two chief towns are Georgetown on the river Demerara, and New Amsterdam on the river Berbice; the former, which is the residence of the Governor, is considered the capital of British Guiana.

Inhabitants.

British Guiana is inhabited by Europeans, Africans, and native Americans. The Europeans are mostly Englishmen and their descendants; very few of the former Dutch settlers having remained in the colony since it was ceded to Great Britain. The Negroes, who were originally brought over from Africa to cultivate the soil, constitute by far the greatest number of the inhabitants. The native Americans have dwindled to an inconsiderable number.

The following statement of the population of British Guiana is given from Parliamentary tables and Montgomery Martin's Statistics of the Colonial Empire. There has been no census of the population in Demerara and Essequibo since 1829.

Population of the Colonies Demerara and Essequibo in 1829.

District.	Whites.			Free Coloured.			Slaves.		
	Males.	Females	Total.	Males.	Females	Total.	Males.	Females	Total.
Demerara in the country.	662	110	772	463	617	1080	33,883	28,869	62,752
Essequibo	476	138	614	442	470	912			
Georgetown	962	658	1620	1625	2743	4368	3,209	3,407	6,616
Total	2100	906	3006	2530	3830	6360	37,092	32,276	69,368

Total population in Demerara and Essequibo in 1829:—41,722 males, 37,012 females; grand total 78,734.

The following census shows the total population of Demerara alone, October 31st, 1829.

No. of Company.	Battalion of Militia.	District.	Whites.			Free Black and Coloured.			Grand total.
			Males.	Females.	Total.	Males.	Females.	Total.	
1	2	From plantation Thomas to plantation Lusignan, parish of St. George and St. Mary	81	7	88	23	42	65	153
2	...	From plantation Annandale to plantation Lancaster, parish of St. Paul and St. Mary	87	1	88	29	37	66	154
3	...	From plantation Cane Grove to Mahaica village, parish of St. Mary	71	10	81	67	113	180	261
4	...	From Abari to plantation Bath, parish of St. Mary	28	3	31	38	74	112	143
1	3	From plantation La Pénitence, including canal No. 3, parish of St. Matthew	82	20	102	36	51	87	189
2	...	From plantation La Grange to plantation Waller's Delight, parish of St. Swithin	52	7	59	33	44	77	136
3	...	From plantation La Parfaite Harmonie to plantation Wales, parish of St. Mark	60	11	71	25	33	58	129
4	...	From plantation Vriesland to Saesdyk, parish of St. Mark and part of St. Matthew	32	2	34	38	46	84	118
5	...	From plantation Sans Souci on the lower side, to Dinabuna on the upper, parishes of St. Mark and St. Matthew	23	9	32	55	51	106	138
6	...	From Windsor Forest to Borasiri Creek, parishes of St. Swithin and St. Luke	80	2	82	25	28	53	135
7	...	From plantation Zeelugt to Beverhauts, parish of St. Luke	35	23	58	37	45	82	140
...	...	From plantation Mara to plantation Loo, Upper Demerara river, parish of St. Luke	31	15	46	57	53	110	156
			662	110	772	463	617	1080	1852

A similar return for Essequibo at the same date gives the population thus:

No. of Company.	Battalion of Militia.	District.	Whites.			Free Black and Coloured.			Grand total.
			Males.	Females.	Total.	Males.	Females.	Total.	
2	1	From Fort Island, inclusive of both sides of the river upwards	9	13	22	61	58	119	141
3	...	Leguan Island and Hog Island, parish of St. Peter	110	32	142	52	51	103	245
4	...	From plantation Caledonia to plantation Maria's Lodge, parish of St. James.........	86	15	101	34	37	71	172
5	...	From Vergeleegen to Aboeneboenaba, parish of St. John	33	13	46	176	186	362	408
1	2	From Caro Caro creek to plantation Hoff van Holland, parish of St. John ..	54	12	66	62	66	128	194
2	...	From plantation Alliance to Cattle Town, parish of St. John............................	63	37	100	28	38	66	166
3	...	From plantation Taymouth Manor to Shamrock Hall	121	16	137	29	34	63	200
			476	138	614	442	470	912	1526

General census and appraisement of Georgetown of the 31st of October, 1829.

District.	White.			Free Black and Coloured.			Grand total.	Appraised value of lots and buildings in 1830.
	Males.	Females.	Total.	Males.	Females.	Total.		
								ƒ.
Kingston	66	68	134	158	277	435	569	508,040
North Cumingsburg	117	85	202	231	359	590	792	1,355,350
South Cumingsburg, including Company Path with respect to appraisement	202	108	310	375	630	1005	1315	1,554,340
Robb's Town	144	32	176	78	135	213	389	1,069,200
NewTown, including Colombia	52	21	73	29	58	87	160	362,000
Stabrook	81	69	150	80	182	262	412	427,350
Werken Rust	148	118	266	316	495	811	1077	778,660
Charlestown	86	84	170	183	299	482	652	407,750
Lacy Town	66	73	139	175	308	483	622	
	962	658	1620	1625	2743	4368	5988	6,462,692

BRITISH GUIANA.

The Slave population in each parish of Demerara and Essequibo, 31st of May, 1832, was:

Parishes.	Males.	Females.	Total.	Births under three years of age.		Births per cent.*	Deaths.
				Males.	Females.		
St. Mary	3394	2907	6301	237	224	$7, \frac{1993}{6301}$	$9, \frac{1891}{6301}$
St. Paul	4510	4262	8772	300	338	$7, \frac{599}{2193}$	$8, \frac{1981}{2193}$
St. George & St. Andrew	3993	4040	8033	280	297	$7, \frac{1469}{8033}$	$7, \frac{7769}{9033}$
St. Matthew	2934	2670	5604	158	162	$5, \frac{995}{1401}$	$11, \frac{238}{467}$
St. Mark	2570	2063	4633	116	108	$4, \frac{3863}{4633}$	$10, \frac{4170}{4633}$
St. Swithin ...	2059	1851	3910	104	104	$5, \frac{125}{391}$	$13, \frac{307}{391}$
St. Luke	2930	2605	5535	167	193	$6, \frac{62}{123}$	$11, \frac{463}{1107}$
St. Peter	3015	2872	5887	178	155	$5, \frac{3865}{5887}$	$13, \frac{969}{5887}$
St. James......	2126	2040	4166	82	106	$4, \frac{1068}{2083}$	$13, \frac{1171}{2083}$
St. John	2471	2146	4617	128	144	$5, \frac{4115}{4617}$	$11, \frac{2813}{4617}$
The Trinity ...	4347	3712	8059	224	281	$6, \frac{2186}{8059}$	$10, \frac{616}{8059}$
	34,349	31,168	65,517	1974	2112		
Slaves attached to plantation	28,083	24,394	53,477	1558	1705		
Personal and unattached	6266	5774	12,040	416	407		

According to these returns, the number of slaves in Demerara and Essequibo on the 31st May 1832, was 65,517; of which

    4,086 were under 3 years of age,
    2,744 above 3 years and not exceeding 5,
    5,401 between 5 and 10,
    6,115 ———— 10 — 16,
    16,013 ———— 16 — 30,

* Since the Registration of May, 1829.

BRITISH GUIANA.

8,345 between 30 and 40,
13,585 ——— 40 — 50,
7,179 ——— 50 — 60,
1,613 ——— 60 — 70,
363 ——— 70 — 80,
40 ——— 80 — 90,
7 ——— 90 — 100,
2 100 years and upwards,
24 age unknown, supposed to be absentees.

Population of the county of Berbice.

The population of Berbice in 1764 was

116 whites.
1,308 male negroes.
1,307 female ditto.
745 children.
————
Total 3,476

Return of the population of the colony of Berbice in October 1827.

District.	Whites.			Free Coloured.			Slaves.		
	Males.	Females.	Total.	Males.	Females.	Total.	Males.	Females.	Total.
New Amsterdam.	130	49	179	324	530	854	695	681	1376
Country.....	289	55	344	130	177	307	10202	8540	18742
Total...	419	104	523	454	707	1161	10897	9221	20118

Total population of the colony of Berbice in 1827, 21,802 souls; showing an increase, if compared with the census of 1764, of 18,326.

The population of this colony according to the return of 1833 was as follows:

District.	Whites.			Free Coloured.			Slaves.		
	Males.	Females.	Total.	Males.	Females.	Total.	Males.	Females.	Total.
Town of New Amsterdam.	161	95	256	527	779	1306	...	...	...
Canje District....	50	5	55	39	35	74	...	...	...
East and Corentyn Coast. ...	51	8	59	14	53	67	...	...	...
West Coast.	53	15	68	13	27	40	...	...	...
River Berbice......	116	16	132	78	86	164	...	...	...
Total ...	431	139	570	671	980	1651	10,243	9,077	19,320

Total population of the colony of Berbice in 1833, 21,541 souls; showing, if compared with the census of 1827, an increase of 47 whites, 490 free coloured, and a decrease in the number of slaves of 798. In the absence of data as to how many slaves bought their freedom during that period the decrease by death cannot be correctly obtained. Between the years 1828 and 1831, 118 slaves received their manumission.

An attempt has been made to ascertain by a general census the population of British Guiana at that remarkable epoch when slavery was abolished throughout the British Colonies. Some difficulties which opposed themselves to such an important step have delayed the result, but it is to be hoped that the execution of a subject so desirable has not been abandoned by the local authorities.

Population of British Guiana.

The number of the negro population in British Guiana, in respect of whom compensation was claimed and awarded under the act for abolishing slavery, was, according to the parliamentary return to the House of Lords,—

Prædial attached	57,807
Prædial non-attached	5,475
Non-prædial	6,297
Total for whom compensation was awarded	69,579
Children under six years of age, Aug. 1, 1834.	9,893
Aged, diseased, or otherwise non-effective.	3,352
Total slave population	82,824

The value put upon the entire slave population, computed from sales between 1822 and 1830, was 9,489,559*l.*; and the compensation paid for the labouring classes out of the twenty millions awarded by parliament, amounted to 4,268,809*l.*, that for the children and aged persons, &c., was 226,180*l.*

The whole population of British Guiana, excluding the Aborigines, probably amounts at present to 98,000* individuals, which gives only one hundred and thirty inhabitants to one hundred square miles.

Indians or aboriginal inhabitants.

History informs us that the discoverers of South America found the continent densely peopled by Indians. What then has become of the millions of aborigines who once inhabited these regions? Driven from their lands, now in possession of the Europeans and their descendants, they have wandered from their ancient homes, strangers in their own country; and diseases and vices introduced by the settlers, and feuds among themselves, have all but annihilated the rightful owners of the soil. It is a melancholy fact, but too well founded, that where-

---

* According to the following estimate:

Negro population as above	82,824
Coloured	8,076
Whites	4,000
Emigrants since 1829	3,100

ever Europeans have settled, the extermination of the native tribes has succeeded their arrival.

Guiana is inhabited by a thinly scattered population of aboriginal natives, who, although they agree in stature and features, in disposition and customs, and mode of living, differ nevertheless in language, and this difference is so great, that tribes who live adjacent to each other speak a language essentially distinct. To ascertain the affinities of these languages is a task of the greatest difficulty, and demands a closer application and a longer period than I have had time to dedicate to it. The analogy in the roots of the Caribi, the Macusi, and the Arecuna; the Wapisiana, and the Parauana, leaves little doubt that these nations descend from the same stock; the Aráwaak, Warrau, Taruma, Woyawai differ more or less in their composition. The Accawai, or Waccawaio, is merely a dialect of the Caribi.

The most powerful tribes now extant are the Macusis and Arecunas, who inhabit the extensive plains on our southern and south-western boundary; but of the Caribi, the once widely-extended people, who retained their independence for a long period after the arrival of the Europeans, and who were the terror of all other nations, there remain but few in British Guiana.

It is difficult, if not impossible, to form an estimate approximating to truth of the number of aborigines within the boundaries of British Guiana. Their wandering life increases this difficulty. They consist of the following tribes:

1. Arawaak.
2. Warrau.
3. Caribi or Caribisi.
4. Accawai or Waccawaio.
5. Taruma.
6. Macusi.
7. Arecuna.
8. Wapisiana.
9. Atorai or Atoria.
10. Woyawai.

The Arawaaks and Warraus live at the coast regions, and their small settlements extend scarcely one hundred miles inland: I estimate their number at 3150. The Caribis inhabit the lower Mazaruni and Cuyuni; about 100 are located at the Corentyn, 80 at the Rupununi, 30 at the Guidaru, and their whole number (once the lords of the soil) does not at present surpass 300. The Accawais or Waccawaios inhabit the upper Demerara, the Mazaruni, and Potaro, and amount likely to 600. The Macusis occupy the open country or savannahs of the Rupununi, Parima, and the mountain chains Pacaraima and Canucu. Those who inhabit our territory number 1500; the whole tribe is probably not less than 3000. They are bordered to the north by the Arecunas, who inhabit the mountainous regions at the head-waters of the Caroni and Cuyuni. They are a powerful tribe, but are more properly the inhabitants of the Venezuelean territory; about 150 live at the south-western tributaries of the Mazaruni. The Wapisiana are a tribe inhabiting the savannahs of the upper Rupununi and the banks of the Parima: I estimate the number who inhabit our territory at 500. The Atorais, at the Carawaima mountains and along their north-western foot, border on the territory of the Wapisiana; the Atorais, like the Caribis, are fast approaching their extinction; their whole number does not amount to 200. The Tarumas * inhabit the tributaries of the upper Essequibo: they are a fine athletic tribe, very likely amounting to not less than 500 individuals. The Woyawais, a race who inhabit the regions between the head waters of the Essequibo and the affluents of the

* Von Martius in his enumeration of Indian tribes considers the Tarumas or Taruman extinguished. It appears they have retreated from the mouth of the Rio Negro, which they formerly inhabited, to the head-waters of the Essequibo.

Amazons, number about 350: they are on the southern confines of our boundary. The aggregate number of Indians in British Guiana is therefore estimated at 7000.

While an account of their manners and customs would be here out of place, their forlorn situation engages all our sympathy. Their present history is the finale of a tragical drama; a whole race of men is wasting away; but heartless is the assertion, unworthy of our philanthropic age, that the indigenous race of the new world is insusceptible of elevation, and that no power of princes, philosophy, or Christianity can arrest its gloomy progress towards certain destruction. Such a heartless idea could not have been adopted by him who lived with them, who studied their character. I speak from experience, if I assert that the Indian is as capable of progressive improvement, and the establishment, among his tribe, of social order, European arts, and Christian morals, as were the Teutonic races in their infancy, who emerged progressively from the greatest barbarism to the bright station which they at present occupy among the most civilized nations of Europe. Let us compare their present condition with the picture which Tacitus drew of the social state and manners of these Germans, and we may yet hope that if proper measures were adopted to raise the Indian from his forlorn situation, these efforts would be crowned equally with success.

The system of the Brazilians of hunting the Indians for slaves exists to this day in all its atrocities. These slaving expeditions, or descimentos, from political motives are always directed towards the contested boundaries; and their practice is, when arrived at a populous Indian village, to await the mantle of the night in ambush, and to fall over their unsuspecting victims when enjoying the

Slavery expeditions of the Brazilians against the Indians.

first sleep. By setting their cabins on fire and discharging their muskets they create consternation, and succeed in securing the greater part of the former peaceful inhabitants. I had thus the grief, while at the Brazilian boundary fort San Joaquim on the Rio Branco, in August 1838, to witness the arrival of a similar expedition, who surprised an Indian village near the Ursato mountains, on the eastern bank of the river Takutu, on the contested boundary of British Guiana, and carried forty individuals, namely, eighteen children under twelve years of age, thirteen women, and nine men, of whom only four were under thirty years of age, and two above fifty, into slavery. These abominable proceedings were carried on under the warrant of the district authorities.

Religious and Public Instruction.

The efforts which the local government and legislative bodies have made in British Guiana to promote religion and education, deserve the highest praise. There are few instances in colonial history, where in so short a time, and under difficulties of no common description, a country has made such rapid progress in the erection and endowment of places of worship and public instruction.

Religious establishment in 1796. In the year 1796*, when the colony was first taken by the English troops, and in 1803, when it again surrendered, the only church in the colony was in Fort Island, with two ministers of religion, namely, the chaplain of the British forces and the minister of the Dutch

* *V.* A charge delivered to the clergy of the English church in British Guiana, the 18th July 1839, by the Right Rev. Bishop of Barbadoes, &c. Demerara, 1839.

reformed church. In 1802 a family having occasion to visit England, were under the necessity of taking their children with them unbaptized, from the want of a pastor to administer the very initiatory sacrament of our religion.

St. George's church was opened for the performance of Divine service in 1810, the colony churches in Georgetown and New Amsterdam in 1819 and 1820, the church of the Holy Trinity in 1825. The colony of Demarara and Essequibo was not divided into parishes until 1824, when there were not more than three clergymen for the religious necessities of a country, which, including Berbice, extended in length alone over a space of more than two hundred and eighty miles. Public schools, with the exception of the Saffon Institution, there were none. It was only at that period, that strenuous efforts were made to improve the heathen and uncivilized state of the colony, and we find that between the years 1824 and 1831, upwards of 350,000 guilders, or about £26,000, were expended on the building of churches and parsonages; independently of which, large sums were voluntarily contributed by individuals for that purpose. On the estimate for the year 1832, a sum of 200,725 guilders, equal to £14,337, was placed for the support of the ecclesiastical establishment of that year alone*. It consisted in 1836 of seven rectors and one curate attached to the established church of England, two ministers to the church of Holland, five ministers to the church of Scotland, two priests to the Roman Catholic church, twelve catechists and schoolmasters. The annual sum paid to the clergymen, catechists, and schoolmasters and schoolmistresses, amounted to 135,450 guilders, equal to about £10,000. These expenses are borne solely by the inhabitants by taxes levied on them, and

Religious establishment in 1836.

* R. Montgomery Martin, British Colonial Library, vol. v. p. 157.

the Roman Catholic clergy are placed on the same footing as the clergy of the established church, or those of the Dutch or Scotch persuasion.

From England, through the bishop of the diocese, there has been received, in 1837, by means of the parliamentary grant or otherwise, about £5000 towards chapels and schools. From the colonial fund, there has been paid in 1837, £3407 towards the erection of schools or the procuring of teachers. The number of persons who received instruction in 1838, in British Guiana, amounted to 11,363, namely, 4683 adults and 6680 children.

British Guiana erected into an archdeaconry: number of churches, school-houses, &c.

In 1838, the province of British Guiana was erected into a separate archdeaconry within the diocese of Barbadoes, and the number of the clergy of the church of England has been increased to eighteen, while the instruction is confided to twenty-eight schoolmasters, exclusive of schoolmistresses, and the ten colonial clerks and catechists. The total number of ecclesiastical buildings in connexion with the established church of England, together with the parish churches appropriated to the use of the kirk of Scotland, amounts to not less than forty-seven, besides eight private estate schools.

The Christians who confess the Roman Catholic faith are now under a titular bishop or vicar apostolic*, to whose establishment five priests and several schools are attached.

I have yet to allude to the eight places of worship and public instruction which are under the care of the Missionaries of the Wesleyan and London Missionary Societies and the Mico Charities, whose faithful activity has produced the best results.

* At present, the Right Reverend Dr. Clanc, Bishop of Oriense, a man generally respected for his worth and learning.

The estimate of the amount required to be raised by taxation in the colony of British Guiana for the service of the year 1839, is 633,366 dollars, 4cts., of which the provision for the respective religious establishments throughout the colony, amounts to 108,975 dollars, (equal to £22,942 sterling) or about the sixth of the whole sum necessary for the public service of the colony for that year.

Guiana sets certainly a bright example for promoting religion and diffusing public instruction throughout the colony. The above sum is only raised by taxation, but numerous are the contributions of communities and private individuals, which are not included in that amount. But if the benevolent of Great Britain should imagine that their pecuniary aid is not more required, they labour under a great mistake: as much as has been done, a great deal is left to be accomplished in order to spread religion and public instruction. The labouring people must not be left in their altered condition to their own resources; and with the avidity which they possess to seek after education, we have an inducement to believe that the negro will be rendered worthy of a state of freedom. The colonists cannot be supposed to have the means of providing any thing approaching to the amount which is necessary to spread religious instruction and moral and intellectual improvement to the required extent among the people, and the realization of this hope depends, therefore, from the benevolent and affluent in Great Britain.

The Indian alone, the owner of the soil which Europeans have usurped, and peopled with the descendants of Africa, he alone is comparatively neglected, and but little care has been evinced to impart to him Christian knowledge, and the adoption of the habits of civilized life. The only attempts which hitherto have been made to *[Mission to the Indians neglected.]*

their conversion since the colony is under the British domain, emanated from the mission at Bartica Point, at the confluence of the Mazaruni with the Essequibo; and the establishment of a Mr. Peters at Caria-Caria on the left bank of the lower Essequibo, whose zealous and disinterested endeavours to preach the Gospel to the aborigines have been so far crowned with success, that he presides now as a religious teacher over a community of about sixty converted natives of the Arawaak nation, who, out of their own means, erected a neat chapel, capable of containing two hundred and fifty people. Their example may serve as another proof of the anxious desire manifested by the Indian to participate in the advantages of civilized life and religious instruction. In 1837, the Indians at the river Marocco, who are mostly emigrants from the former catholic missions at the Caroni, were given under the charge of a Roman catholic priest.

Failure of a protestant mission to the Macusi Indians, in consequence of Brazilian interference.

A mission to the Macusi Indians promised great success. A protestant clergyman, the Rev. Mr. Youde, settled at Pirara, a village at our undetermined south-western boundary, and the Indians in the neighbourhood soon collected around him, and evinced the greatest anxiety to be instructed in the word of God, and our language. I have seen from three to four hundred Indians on a Sabbath, dressed according to their circumstances, and in an orderly manner, assembled within a rude house of prayer built by their own hands, to receive instruction in the holy word of God. The mission was not established many months, when the Brazilian government of the upper and lower Amazon despatched a detachment of militia, and took possession of the mission under the plea that the village belonged to the Brazilian territory. The missionary of the church of England was accused of having alienated the Indians from the Brazilian government, and instructed them in the English language and religion, and received an injunction to leave the village. The Indians, fearing the Brazilians might conduct them into slavery, dispersed in the forest and in the mountains, and the work which promised such favourable results was destroyed.

It is to be hoped that the spiritual and temporal destitution of the aborigines in British Guiana may obtain the consideration of this government. But few are left of those races, who at the first arrival of Europeans densely peopled this vast continent. Would it not be worthy of an enlightened government, not only on religious, but likewise on political grounds, to advise some plan for the amelioration of their forlorn situation? Like the African, they are the descendants of our common parent, and have the same claim upon our pity and protection.

Public Income and Expenditure.

The revenue, on an average of four years, of Demerara and Essequibo amounts to £70,000, and of Berbice to £20,000; the total expenditure in Demerara and Essequibo to £65,000, in Berbice to £18,000. These sums do not include an item of £45,000, incurred for military protection. The revenue and expenditure of the colony is, however, more distinctly learned from the subsequent table.

The expenditure for 1839 was estimated, for the counties Demerara and Essequibo at £73,912; for the county Berbice, £29,944, which sum was to be raised by a tax on produce; a tax on an annual income of 500 dollars and upwards; duties upon all importations not being of the origin or manufacture of Great Britain; a tax on horses and carriages, colony crafts of all descriptions, cart licenses, shooting or gun licenses, hucksters' licenses, wine and spirit duties, liquor licenses, tonnage and bacon duty*. Tax on transient traders, &c., &c.

The civil list or expenditure, for salaried officers of the colonial government and courts of justices, &c., amounts, for British Guiana, to £19,592, of which sum the counties of Demerara and Essequibo pay three quarters, and the county Berbice one quarter. Berbice, which continues with a distinct staff of government, has a separate estimate, which causes the inhabitants of that county to be more highly taxed than those in Demarara and Essequibo, and which in some instances amounted to three hundred per cent. above that of the latter counties.

Revenue and Expenditure of the Colony of British Guiana.

Year.	Demerara & Essequibo.		Berbice.		Total.	
	Revenue.	Expenditure.	Revenue.	Expenditure.	Revenue.	Expenditure.
	£	£	£	£	£	£
1833	47,273	38,997	23,239	16,331	70,512	55,328
1834	81,417	45,923	20,847	18,503	102,164	64,426
1835	53,359	55,075	14,208	16,634	67,267	71,709
1836	87,885	97,371	18,196	16,575	106,081	113,946

Later details are wanting; the receipts in the office of the Colonial Receiver for the counties Demerara and Essequibo amounted, from the 1st of January until the 30th of June, 1838, to £27,660 4s., and for the same period in 1839 to £32,389 14s., showing an excess of £4729 10s. as compared with 1838, although there is a diminution of £6557 7s. in the item of import duties, in consequence of the import duties on British manufactures having been disallowed by the Home Government since July 1838. The rum duty for the six months, from the 1st of January to the 30th of June, netted £4288 15s.

* Forty cents per ton. The seamen are entitled, if sick, to go to the seamen's hospital, free of any charge to the ship.

The coins current in the colony are British half-crowns, shillings, and sixpenny pieces, colonial silver coinage, and Spanish dollars, half-dollars, and quarter-dollars. *Monetary system.*

The colonial coinage consists of three-guilder, two-guilder, and one-guilder pieces, and $\frac{1}{2}$, $\frac{1}{4}$, $\frac{1}{8}$ guilder pieces. There are no colonial gold or copper coins in circulation.

The paper currency of Demerara and Essequibo, which, in 1832, amounted to 2,199,758 guilders, equal to £157,126, was secured on funded property and colonial security. The necessary orders have been given by the colonial government for its redemption. The amount of paper currency in circulation in Berbice amounted on the 31st December, 1834, to 426,099 guilders, equal to £30,436, not secured on funded property, but merely on the ordinary and extraordinary revenue of the colony. This sum has offered therefore a serious impediment for having only one estimate for the colony of British Guiana, and an equalization of the taxes of Berbice to those of Demerara and Essequibo. This object has been happily accomplished, and the redemption of the paper currency is to be effected by the acre money and the sale of the second depth of land.

The par of exchange is 12 guilders per pound sterling, but of late years it has been fluctuating between 13fl. and 15fl. The rate of exchange in all government or public transactions is fixed at 14fl. per pound sterling. According to an ordinance of the legislative council, accounts are now kept in dollars and cents, at the rate of 4s. 4d. sterling for the dollar.

There is, in the colony, a branch of the West India Colonial Bank, and a local establishment called the British Guiana Bank. The latter consists of six thousand shares at 700 guilders (equal to £50 sterling) each, which have all been taken up by parties within the colony, and *Banks.*

fifty per cent. had been paid up thereon in June 1838. The prosperous state of the bank may be learned from the report published at the half-yearly meeting in January 1840, according to which an interest of upwards of eleven and a half per cent. per annum had been realized on the bank's paid-up capital stock, of which, however, only four per cent. for the half year were paid up, leaving the balance for the reserved funds. The chief offices of both banks are in Georgetown, with branches in New Amsterdam.

Weights and measures. Principally steelyards from 1 to 3500lbs. are used for weighing; there is a difference of 10 per cent. between Dutch and English weights, namely 110lbs. Dutch = 100lbs. English. The English yard is generally adopted as long measure; the Dutch ell of 26 inches Rhynland is equal to 27 inches English. The English gallon is the fluid measure in use.

The property annually created by the productions of the land, animal food, and fish, merchandize, made, &c., is estimated at £3,789,166; the property moveable and immoveable, including uncultivated land, public property, as forts, wharfs, churches, forts, barracks, roads,* canals, &c., at £24,020,000. The abstract appraisement of Georgetown amounted, in 1836, to £586,934, in 1839 to £712,969, showing an increase of the value of buildings and lots in three years of £132,035.

Staple Products and Commerce.

The staple products of the colony consist of sugar, rum, coffee and cotton.

The following historical records and tables exhibit the state of cultivation of British Guiana at different periods.

The first record which we possess of the produce ex-

* Full 250 miles of public roads, averaging £600 a mile.—Montgomery Martin's History of the West Indies, vol. ii. p. 173.

ported from the colonies Essequibo and Demerara, consisted, in 1747, of 559 tierces, or half-hogsheads, of sugar, which were carried to Europe in two schooners. About this time there must have been a great influx of labourers, as the export rose the subsequent year (1748) to 2292 hogsheads of sugar. In 1752, they commenced to cultivate cotton and coffee, but the export amounted only to one bale of cotton and one bag of coffee. The exports in 1761 were only 878 hogsheads of sugar, 28 bales of cotton, and 45 tierces of coffee.

In 1764 the total number of estates under cultivation on the banks of the rivers Essequibo and Demerara, consisted of 130, which produced that year $2956\frac{1}{2}$ hogsheads of sugar, 211 bags of coffee, and two bales of cotton, which produce was sent in eight ships to Europe.

In 1773 the exports amounted to 8613 bags, and 181 bales of cotton, 3775 hogsheads of sugar, and 1001 tierces of coffee.

In 1775 19,090 bags and 189 bales of cotton, 2317 tierces of coffee, and 4939 hogsheads of sugar were exported.

In 1796, General Whyte, with three British regiments, took possession of Demerara and Essequibo, and under the protection of Great Britain, agriculture and commerce made rapid progress; and such was the effect of British capital and enterprise, that, in 1803, consequently seven years after having been taken possession of, the exports were raised to 19,638 hogsheads, 213 tierces, and 161 barrels of sugar; 4887 puncheons of rum; 46,435 bales of cotton; 9,954,610lbs. of coffee; and 311 casks of molasses; requiring 394 vessels for their transport. Twenty years after, namely in 1823, the exports consisted of 51,360 hogsheads, 449 tierces, 2470 barrels of sugar; 15,781 puncheons, 2568 hogsheads of rum; 9587 bales of cotton; 8,084,729lbs. of coffee; 19,634 hogsheads, 230 tierces, and 269 barrels of molasses, and although the number of vessels which were required to transport this produce to Europe amounted only to 368, consequently 26 less than in 1803, we may suppose that their tonnage was much heavier.

The following return, given on oaths, shows the productions of Demerara and Essequibo, for periods of three years each.

Years.	Sugar.	Coffee.	Cotton.
	lbs. Dutch.*	lbs.	lbs.
1823-24-25	213,478,633	17,779,473	6,808,913
1826-27-28	239,556,975	13,897,083	7,389,373
1829-30-31	262,709,559	7,059,431	2,252,557

It will be observed, that while sugar has been cultivated during the last three years to a greater extent, coffee and cotton have been neglected.

The following tables exhibit the number of estates in British Guiana, in 1831, 1832 and in 1839.

DEMERARA AND ESSEQUIBO.

Parishes.	Number of Estates in May, 1832.						
	Sugar	Sugar and Coffee	Cotton	Coffee	Coffee and Cotton	Timber	Farms
St. Mary	18	0	5	0	1	0	7
St. Paul	14	3	6	0	2	0	1
St. George and St. Andrew	4	1	0	4	0	0	0
St. Matthew	6	11	0	5	0	0	0
St. Mark	11	3	0	16	0	2	0
St. Swithin	2	9	0	2	0	0	0
St. Luke	13	6	0	3	0	2	2
St. Peter	28	0	0	0	0	1	0
St. James	20	0	0	0	0	1	0
St. John	18	2	0	1	0	2	0
Trinity	20	1	1	2	1	1	0
Total number ...	154	36	12	33	4	9	10

* 112lbs. Dutch equal to 112lbs. 4oz. avoirdupois.

BRITISH GUIANA.

Parishes.	Number of Estates in December 1839.			Remarks.
	Sugar.	Coffee and plantains.	Cotton and plantains.	
St. Mary	18	3	6	Ninety-four lots entirely uncultivated.
St. Paul	17	0	9	Seven uncultivated, which have been previously in cotton.
St. George and St. Andrew	4	2	0	
St. Matthew.........	16	9	0	Fifteen lots either abandoned, or cultivated with plantains to a small extent.
St. Mark	13	17	0	Forty-four lots either abandoned, or affording a small supply of firewood.
St. Swithin	14	0	0	
St. Luke	17	2	0	Fifteen entirely abandoned, a few only with a limited cultivation of plantains.
St. Peter	27	0	0	
St. James............	20	0	0	Six abandoned.
St. John	20	4	0	
Trinity	19	6	0	The six in the second column are partly in coffee, partly in cotton and plantains.
Total	185	40	15	

BERBICE.

Comparative table of the number of Estates in cultivation in Berbice during the years 1831 and 1839.

District.	Number of Estates.					
	Sugar.		Coffee.		Cotton.	
	1831.	1839.	1831.	1839.	1831.	1839.
West sea-coast of Berbice ...	6	7	0	0	5	2
West side of Berbice river ...	3	6	18	15	0	0
East side of Berbice river ...	6	8	19	14	0	0
West side of Cauje creek ...	2	2	5	4	0	0
East side of Cauje creek......	6	6	1	0	0	0
East coast canal	2	2	0	0	0	0
East coast	0	0	0	0	2	0
Corentyn coast	6	6	0	0	2	2
Total	31	37	43	33	9	4

The subsequent table exhibits the produce made in British Guiana during the stated periods, and rests upon government returns.

BRITISH GUIANA.

A statement of the quantity of produce made in the following years.

Year.	Sugar in lbs.	Rum in gals.	Molasses in gals.	Coffee in lbs.	Cotton in lbs.	Value of plantains and cattle sold in £.
1832	96,381,959	2,820,594	4,502,473	6,410,535	1,157,709	44,900
1833	99,106,827	2,516,138	5,121,301	4,490,596	954,957	56,910
1834	81,085,483	2,631,630	3,288,586	3,035,556	926,944	37,980
1835	107,586,405	3,743,687	3,105,421	3,065,742	867,942	41,230
1836	107,806,249	2,980,296	4,035,569	5,875,732	656,902	....
1837	99,851,195	1,975,260	3,405,906	4,066,200	803,200	....
1838	88,664,885	2,068,052	3,132,675	3,143,543	641,920	....

A statement of the quantity of produce made in 1833 and 1836 in Demerara and Essequibo, and in Berbice, respectively.

Produce.	Demerara and Essequibo.		Berbice.	
	1833.	1836.	1833.	1836.
Sugar in lbs.	87,248,821	85,982,756	11,858,006	21,823,493
Rum in gallons	2,187,234	2,348,920	339,398	631,376
Molasses in gallons.........	4,636,294	3,491,991	485,007	543,578
Coffee in lbs.	2,587,744	2,635,741	1,871,852	3,239,991
Cotton in lbs.	538,126	466,078	416,731	190,824

The exports of the products in 1836 were made to various countries, in the following proportions.

Countries.	Sugar.			Rum.			Cotton.	Coffee.	Molasses.
	Hogsheads.	Tierces.	Barrels.	Puncheons.	Hogsheads.	Barrels.	Bales.		Casks.
United Kingdom	65,448	4348	3814	19,778	5202	1605	3176	1,489,550 lbs. 3033 tierces 1429 bags	29,278
British N. American Colonies	456	97	144	5312	251	37	......	450 lbs. 6 bags	6402
British West Indies	1179	59	6	2057	93	......	339	7300 lbs. 35 tierces 10 bags	1377
Foreign Countries	411	173	34	954	88	5	......	208,450 lbs.	1726
Total	67,494	4677	3998	28,101	5634	1647	3515	1,705,750 lbs. 3068 tierces 1445 bags	38,783
Total value	1,529,918£			157,003£			40,149£	247,444£	160,865£

Grand Total..................2,135,379£.

The exports of British Guiana for the year 1839, including the exports from Berbice to 18th December, 1839, amount to

 35,845 hogsheads, 2135 tierces, 2396 barrels of sugar.
 13,245 puncheons, 3817 hogsheads, 882 barrels of rum.
 11,664 casks, 85 hogsheads, 14 barrels of molasses.
1,356,700 lbs. of coffee.
 912 bales of cotton.

Showing a decrease, as compared with 1838, of

 12,967 hogsheads of sugar.
 2340 puncheons, 234 hogsheads, 855 barrels of rum.
 11,302 casks of molasses.
1,738,790 lbs. of coffee.
 197 bales of cotton.

But if the exports of 1839 be compared with those of 1836, (for which comparison the preceding table of exports to the various countries affords the necessary data,) we find the frightful decrease of—

31,649 hogsheads ⎫
  2542 tierces   ⎬ sugar valued at £665,748
  1602 barrels   ⎭

14,856 puncheons ⎫
  1817 hogsheads ⎬ rum valued at £240,436
   765 barrels   ⎭

2603 bales of cotton, valued at £31,236

3668 tierces ⎫
1445 bags   ⎬ coffee valued at £98,926

11,302 puncheons of molasses valued at £113,020

} at the present prices of colonial produce:

which deficiency of produce amounts to nearly 1,150,000*l.*, an item of sufficient importance to attract the attention of every one who is interested in the welfare of the British colonies. The decrease of duties to the Exchequer, in 1839, arising from produce cultivated in British Guiana, if compared with 1836, must have amounted to 1,500,000*l.* These duties amounted in 1833 to 2,728,661*l.*

The actual amount of the value of British and foreign goods shipped to British Guiana will be indicated by the following table.

Year.	British Goods.			Amount of all imports in British Guiana, British and Foreign.
	Demerara and Essequibo.	Berbice.	Total Amount.	
	£	£	£	£
1832	337,263	50,936	338,199	573,195
1833	337,482	54,038	391,520	557,574
1834	410,764	52,687	463,451	853,628
1835	439,773	71,588	511,361	615,106
1836	770,839	140,738	911,577	1,204,560

I have not been able to procure later details with regard to imports in British Guiana. In July 1838 the import duties on British goods were disallowed, and their importation does not rest on authentic returns. But the increasing consumption of imports by the mass of the population renders an estimate of 1,500,000*l.* for the amount of all imports by no means improbable.

Statement of the Shipping employed in the trade of the Shipping.
colonies Demerara and Essequibo, and Berbice.

Year.	Inwards.						Outwards.					
	Demarara and Essequibo.			Berbice.			Demarara and Essequibo.			Berbice.		
	Vessels.	Tons.	Men.	Vessels.	Tons.	Men.	Vessels.	Tons.	Men.	Vessels.	Tons.	Men.
1831	601	89,760	5381	342	21,208	1385	563	85,867	5035	246	20,128	1409
1832	571	84,166	5003	318	25,790	1725	567	82,688	4873	338	26,324	1785
1833	633	93,809	5554	289	23,073	1573	620	93,972	5623	312	24,390	1686
1834	630	90,221	5377	286	20,571	1459	616	86,933	5198	294	20,753	1485
1836	543	88,909	5245	173	22,516	1340	543	92,064	5333	185	23,941	1435

In the absence of any detailed information for later years the subsequent table is given.

PORT OF GEORGETOWN, DEMERARA.

An account of the number and tonnage of vessels entered inwards and cleared outwards in the years 1837 and 1838, distinguishing vessels with cargoes from those in ballast.

Year.	Inwards.				Outwards.			
	With Cargoes.		In Ballast.		With Cargoes.		In Ballast.	
	No.	Tons.	No.	Tons.	No.	Tons.	No.	Tons.
1837	502	89,348	30	1083	378	70,160	128	15,873
1838	505	93,618	31	1206	310	60,407	229	35,152

Although the increasing demand of British Guiana for manufactured goods and other supplies has occasioned an additional tonnage inwards, the number of vessels outwards in ballast, it cannot be denied, is but too true a criterion of the deficiency of export. The tonnage inwards was in 1833 for Georgetown 93,800 tons, outwards 94,000 tons; and it is officially acknowledged that the real decrease in the outward tonnage in 1838 as compared with 1837 was about 10,000 tons.

The number of vessels built in the colony of British Guiana from 1814 to 1837, amounted in

    Demerara and Essequibo to 132 or 4717 tons.

    Berbice . . . . 23 or 1015 tons.

The comparatively small number of vessels built in the colony, where the indigenous woods insure such advantages for naval architecture, is solely to be ascribed to the want of labour, which renders the expenses too high to afford much inducement to construct even the vessels which are wanted for the carrying-trade between the plantations and the ports of Demerara and Berbice in the colony itself.

There are at present four steam-boats in the colony. The largest, which belongs to the local Steam Navigation Company, is of ninety-horse power, and plies between Georgetown and New Amsterdam in Berbice, and the islands in the mouth of the Essequibo and the coast west of that river. Another of twenty-five-horse power plies between the island Leguan, in the mouth of the river Essequibo, and Georgetown. A smaller steamer is employed as a ferry-boat between Georgetown and the western shore of the river Demerara; and the fourth is attached to the extensive wood-cutting establishment of Mr. Patterson, at Christiansburg, in the river Demerara.

A railroad from Georgetown to Mahaica has been projected for some time past, and the actual survey for its construction has already taken place; but the plan has not advanced further as yet. The Lamahak canal, by which not only Georgetown receives a supply of fresh and wholesome water, but which affords likewise irrigation to a number of plantations, deserves notice as a highly useful public work.

Form of Government, Civil Constitution, &c., of the Colony.

Previously to 1831 Berbice continued to be a separate colony, having its own chief magistrate, its civil and criminal courts, and its own current money; but on July 21, 1831, the colonies of Demerara, Essequibo, and Berbice were united into one colony, under the name of British Guiana; and Major General Sir Benjamin D'Urban was the first governor of these united provinces.

The civil government is vested in the governor and court of policy, according to forms which prevailed when the colony was acquired by Great Britain. This supreme court, or colonial parliament, consists of the governor, the chief justice, attorney general, collector of Her Majesty's Customs, and government secretary *ex officiis*, and an equal number of unofficial persons elected from the colonists by the college of electors or kiezers.

The college of electors consists of seven members, who are elected by the inhabitants for life. The votes are sent into the government secretary's office, deposited in a sealed box, and opened in the presence of the governor and not less than two other members of the court of policy. The qualification of electors was formerly the possession of twenty-five slaves; it is at present possessed by every person who pays taxes to the amount of five pounds sterling. <small>College of electors.</small>

In case of vacancies the college of electors nominates two candidates, from which the court selects one as sitting member; which nomination is notified in the Gazette. The unofficial or colonial members of the court of policy serve for three years, and go out by rotation. One or more must vacate his seat every year, but they may be re-elected. The governor, as president of the court of policy, has a casting-vote; every member has a vote. Independently of his having a casting-vote in the decision of all matters under discussion, the governor has an absolute veto on all laws and ordinances that may be passed by a majority; and no ordinance can have the effect of law until it has his approval. The Queen in council may enact or disallow any law.

<small>College of financial representatives.</small>
The college of financial representatives consists of six members, chosen by the inhabitants, like the electors; their term of service is two years.

The court of policy decides on all financial regulations; but when they have prepared an estimate of the expenses for the year, and the mode of taxation and the different items have been discussed and acceded to by a majority, the estimates are handed over to the financial representatives, who in concert with the court of policy examine the charges. In the combined court, every member, whether of the court of policy or financial representatives, has an equal vote. The court of policy combined with the financial representatives having approved of and sanctioned the ways and means, they are passed into law.

<small>Judicial department.</small>
The supreme court of civil justice in British Guiana consists of a chief justice, two puisne judges, a secretary of the chief justice, a registrar, and a sworn accountant. All causes for civil actions and debt are in the first instance heard in what is called the rolls court, before one of the judges, who reports his opinion to the whole court. That court either confirms or rejects this judge's decision. If the cause of action exceeds the value of five hundred pounds sterling, an appeal from the decision of the supreme court lies to the Queen in council.

The laws of Holland, but particularly the laws, statutes, and resolutions of the States-general, are to be followed by the judges of the court in giving judgement.

The supreme court of criminal justice is composed of the three judges of the civil court, and of three assessors, qualified by certain regulations, and drawn by ballot from the box in which the names of all who may have been summoned as assessors are deposited by the clerk of the court: they are however open to challenge by the accused person. These assessors sit on the bench, and the six decide, by the majority of their votes, on the guilt or innocence of the accused person, the casting-vote resting with the chief justice. The sentence must be delivered in open court; and the vote of guilty or not guilty of each individual, whether judge or assessor, is publicly recorded.

The inferior criminal courts are held by the high sheriff of British Guiana at Georgetown, and in Essequibo and Berbice by the sheriffs of these districts or counties.

The sheriff, as chairman, and three magistrates constitute an inferior criminal court; and they can decide on all cases of petty larceny and misdemeanors, but in many instances the sheriff is the sole judge. Not less than three inferior courts are required by law to be held in each county every month.

By virtue of the Act which dissolved slavery, certain tribunals were constituted to decide in matters of dispute between the labourer and the employed, and over which special magistrates are appointed to preside, who receive their appointment from the home government: these tribunals are continued under the new system, and there are thirteen special justices and a circuit magistrate in British Guiana, with a number of constables to assist them in the execution of their duty.

The regulation of the intercourse of the aboriginal inhabitants with the colony, their preservation, and the promotion of their welfare, were formerly vested in six protectors, six postholders, and three assistants. These have been substituted by three superintendents of rivers and creeks, and six postholders. The Indians are little benefited by the present management, and the establishment executes the functions of a police in the interior, rather than effects the purposes avowed when in 1794 the protectors and postholders were called into existence.

Police establishment. The police establishment consists of an inspector-general of British Guiana, and a clerk; two sub-inspectors for the counties Demerara and Essequibo, and one sub-inspector for the county of Berbice; fifteen serjeants and one hundred and five constables for the counties of Demerara and Essequibo; and six serjeants and thirty-two constables for the county of Berbice.

Jails. There are four jails in Demerara and Essequibo, namely, in Georgetown, Mahaica, Wakenaam, and Capoey, one each; and four in the county of Berbice, namely, in New Amsterdam, in the parish of St. Clement and St. Catherine, in the parish of St. Michael, and in the parish St. Saviour.

State of crime. The number of offenders brought before the tribunals during the years 1833, 1834, 1836, is contained in the following table.

Counties.	Years.	Number of Prisoners.	Number of Debtors.	Number of Misdemeanors.	Number of Felons.	Number of tried Prisoners.	Number of untried Prisoners.	Deaths.
Demerara and Essequibo.	1833	156	6	126	24	44	6	2
	1834	2513	10	1926	11	1937	576	1
	1836	2411	6	2380	25	1729	682	1
Berbice.	1833	32	—	28	—	2	2	—
	1834	396	—	393	3	—	—	—
	1836	344	1	32	2	276	68	—

Military defence. All white and other free male inhabitants between the age of sixteen and forty-five were formerly compelled to serve in the militia, but since the abolition of slavery the militia laws were abrogated, and the colonial militia has been since disbanded. The garrison consists at present of a regiment of the line (the 76th) and a detachment of the first West India regiment. The entrance to the port of Demerara is protected by Fort Frederick William, and to the port of Berbice by three batteries, two on the eastern side, and the other, called York redoubt, on the western bank opposite Crab Island. In 1739 an attempt was made to build a fort at Crab Island, but this was found impracticable. A strong battery has been erected at the junction of the Canje. The inconsiderable depth of water along the coast, and the nature of the tides and muddy shores, are the best defence along its coast-line.

Towns and Villages.

GEORGETOWN, the capital of British Guiana, formerly called Stabroek, is situated in latitude 6° 49' 20" N. and longitude 58° 11' 30" W. on the eastern or right bank of the river Demerara, and has a population of not less than 20,000 inhabitants*, of which about 16,000 are coloured. If we except Water-street, which is built close to the river, the streets are wide, traversed by canals; the houses erected of wood, seldom above two stories high; before them are verandas and porticoes, shaded by a projecting roof. They are generally surrounded by a garden or large trees, and separated from each other by canals or trenches. A small fortification built of mud and facines is called Fort William Frederick, and is a short distance from the mouth of the river Demerara, and within a mile of the town; to the eastward of it is

* It has been asserted, that the number of inhabitants in Georgetown amounted, according to the late census, to 25,000; but as the results of this census have not as yet been made public, I give that number merely as a report.

Camp-house, the residence of the officer commanding the troops. In the vicinity of Camp-house are placed two large hospitals, with kitchens, cisterns, &c. for the military, nearly opposite to which Eve Leary barracks have been erected, which for commodiousness are not surpassed in any other colony. The ordnance department, the quarters of the engineers, and the York and Albany barracks are further eastward. The lighthouse with the telegraph is situated between Fort Frederick William and Kingston district.

Georgetown was until lately divided into seven districts, namely, Kingston, North and South Cumingsburgh, Vlissingen, subdivided into Rob's Town and Lacey's town, Stabroek, Werk-en-Rust, and Charlestown; and the care and superintendence was vested in a committee entitled the board of police for Georgetown. It is now divided into eleven wards, in each of which a town councillor is selected by the inhabitants: the town councillors select a mayor. The mayor and town council have the management of the town funds, and form a court for the trial of petty offences committed within the district of the town.

The seat of government was formerly at the Island Borselen, but it was removed in 1774 to the east point of the river Demerara, and named Stabroek, which until 1812 was the general name for Georgetown. It formed a street running from the river towards the forest, and consists still of two rows of houses about a mile long. Facing the river, and within its district, is the new public building, which comprizes all the public offices. This building, which was erected of bricks and stuccoed, cost the colony upwards of 50,000*l.* sterling. The Scotch church, the market-house and the town guard-house are in the vicinity of the public buildings. A new and handsome church of brick in the Gothic style, estimated to cost not less than 13,000*l.* sterling, is now in the course of erection on the site of St. George's church, the parish church of the capital. Christ church, a handsome building on the parade ground, in which a duly licensed minister of the Episcopalian church officiates, was erected upon shares. The Catholic congregation possess a church at Stabroek, which, since the erection of British Guiana into a vicariat apostolic under a titular bishop of Oriense, has been enlarged and formed into a cathedral. The Wesleyan congregation possess a chapel for public worship. There are two public schools in the parish of St. George, one for boys and one for girls; an infant school, and a school of the Mico charity, besides eight private schools. Two public papers, the Gazette and the Guiana Chronicle, are published on alternate days, each three times a week, and the publication of a third is just about being accomplished. Scientific institutions have from time to time been projected, but they perished either in the bud, or if they were established, they lingered a miserable existence and died a natural death. A spirit of apathy pervades the colonists with regard to the encouragement of scientific discoveries and inquiries. An amateur theatre was erected in 1828 in Charlestown by a subscription of several Dutch gentlemen, and in which, since it has become private property, theatrical representations or concerts, by amateurs or professional persons, have continued to be given from time to time. Two horse-races which generally take place towards the commencement and in the middle of the year contribute to the amusements, the more since they end in a well-attended ball. The frequency of private parties and balls may be conceived from the acknowledged hospitality of the West Indians. The colonial hospital is not adequate for the want of the colony, nor can its site be considered healthy.

It is, however, the intention of the local government to erect a new colonial hospital on another site; and a large sum has been voted by the legislature for that purpose. An hospital for the reception of sick seamen possesses every comfort; both institutions are placed under the superintendence of a physician of high standing. The bank for savings of labourers is under the superintendence of the governor and court of policy, and has produced happy results. It has been already stated that the two commercial banks in Guiana have their chief offices in Georgetown.

The shops and stores in Georgetown are very numerous, and offer every article which a European accustomed to luxury or refinement could desire; nor is there a want of the necessary articles for dress for the poorer classes, or the tools of the tradesman, which are to be obtained at so comparatively low a price that there is little or no difference between England and Demerara. Indeed many objects of English manufacture, as glass, paper, tobacco, refined sugar, &c., will be found cheaper in Demerara than in England, in consequence of there being neither home nor colonial duty on those articles, or on any other of English manufacture.

The market is well attended, and the average price of the best beef is about 8$d.$ per pound, mutton 1$s.$ 6$d.$, pork 9$d.$, wheat bread 4$\frac{1}{2}d.$ the pound loaf. Fish and poultry are comparatively high; the labourers when in the state of slavery attended more to the raising of stock than they do now, and a good fowl cannot be had under 4$s.$ The vegetable market offers lettuce, cucumbers, French beans, spinage, asparagus, &c., and the fruit market all the variety and delicacies of a tropical climate. A new and comfortable market-house is in the course of erection. A clerk with some inferior officers attends to the necessary regulations for insuring order during the market hours, and to watch over the common interests. It may be noted as a happy sign, that Sunday markets, which until then had existed, were abolished in October 1839.

NEW AMSTERDAM, the capital of the colony of Berbice before it was united to Demerara and Essequibo, was commenced in 1796; the position of the former town of New Amsterdam, which was higher up, being found inconvenient, the colonists removed nearer to the mouth of the river Berbice, where a little above the junction of the Canje they laid the foundation to the present town. A fort had been built here as early as 1720. The town* extends at present for about a mile and a half along the Berbice, and is intersected by canals. Each house has an allotment of a quarter of an acre of land, generally insulated by trenches, which being filled and emptied with the tide prevent the accumulation of filth. The population amounted in 1833 to 2900 souls; the results of the present census have not transpired as yet. New Amsterdam affords a pretty aspect when entered from seaward. Crab Island is a short distance from the embouchure of the river, and occupies the mid-channel. It is low and bushy, and about a mile in circumference. From its northern and southern point extends a spit of sand, dividing the bed of the river into two navigable channels, of which the eastern has a depth of seventeen to twenty feet, the western only of eight to thirteen feet at high water. The island increases rapidly on its southern point, extending towards the eastern bank of the river, and threatens the destruction of the deeper channel.

* According to my observations, Mr. Sheriff Whinfield's house is in lat. 6° 15′ N. and long. 57° 27′ W.

Opposite Crab Island, and on the river's eastern bank, is the old Fort St. Andrew, a small low fortification, which consisted formerly of four bastions surrounded by a ditch and mounted with eighteen twelve-pounders. It is now in ruins; but its situation for defence is well selected, as an extensive swamp lies in the rear, and being separated from New Amsterdam by the river Canje, it cannot be commanded from any adjacent point. The barracks for the military and the quarters for the engineers and ordnance department, are erected on the junction of the Canje, and occupy a square, which is ballisaded and defended by a strong battery. There are three churches in New Amsterdam; namely, an Episcopalian, which has just been finished, a Scotch church, and a Lutheran church. The English and Scotch services were formerly held alternately in the only colony church which until lately the colony possessed. The Lutheran church, in which service is performed in the Dutch language, possesses the finest organ in British Guiana. The Catholic congregation have their chapel and ministers, and the Wesleyans had already a religious establishment in this town when the colony of Berbice laboured under every other spiritual destitution. There is a free school, which was formerly supported by voluntary contributions; the colonial government has of late assisted in defraying its expenses; there are besides eight private schools. A public paper, the Berbice Advertiser, is published twice a week. Theatrical performances, which have been lately established, contribute to the public amusements. The courthouse, opposite the Scotch church, is a spacious building erected of wood in which the different courts of justice hold their sessions. The commercial part of the town, with commodious wharfs and warehouses to land and receive the goods, fronts the river. The British

Guiana and the Colonial Bank have branch offices in New Amsterdam, and facilitate commerce. A new market-house has just been projected, and is no doubt by this time in the course of building. The town of New Amsterdam was healthy during the period the calamitous endemic disease prevailed in Georgetown. The tide has here free access to the wharfs, which are built upon piles, and thus the accumulation of filth is prevented*.

A ferry-boat plies between the town and the opposite bank of the river. Besides the opportunity which the steamer affords twice a week between Georgetown and New Amsterdam, an overland mail has been established to facilitate the communication between the two chief towns of British Guiana.

The village MAHAICA, built on the west bank of the river of Mahaica, with a few houses on its eastern bank, is the most thriving village in the rural districts of British Guiana. It possesses a church, a Wesleyan chapel, an apothecary's shop, and several stores for the sale of merchandize. The number of houses is estimated at eighty, with a population of six hundred souls.

The hamlet MAHAICONI, on the small river of the same name, consists of about thirty houses, with tradesmen and shops of different descriptions. Some settlements are springing up near the small river Abari; and as the high road from Georgetown to New Amsterdam leads through these villages, they are chiefly recommendable for industrious emigrants.

FREDERICKSBURGH, on the island Wakenaam, with

* While the above has been going through the press colony papers have come to hand which contain the opening speech of the Governor at the Colonial Legislature of 1840, in which he alludes to the same circumstance as the cause of the late prevailing sickness in Georgetown, which I mentioned p. 22.

several mercantile stores, and an apothecary's shop, is greatly increasing.

WILLIAMSTOWN, on the west coast of the river Essequibo, with fifteen houses, a good mercantile store, a church capable of holding five hundred persons, &c. The houses are principally inhabited by tradesmen of all colours.

About seven miles higher up is a village called CATHARINESBURG, with about fifteen houses, a Wesleyan chapel, a store, and an apothecary's shop.

Sixty-three emancipated labourers bought lately, for ten thousand dollars, the abandoned estate of Northbrok, on the east coast of Demerara, where they intend to found a village under the name of VICTORIA, as a token of gratitude and some memento of the emancipation which the purchasers witnessed and enjoyed. They were enabled to pay the purchase money principally from out of their savings since they obtained their freedom.

According to official returns, the number of new stores for the sale of dry goods, provisions, liquors, and merchandise in general, erected and established in the rural districts since the 1st of August, 1838, amounted in fourteen months to seventy-four; the number of settlers' cottages, for the same period, to two hundred and sixty-seven.

BRIEF HISTORICAL RECORDS

OF THE PRESENT COLONY OF BRITISH GUIANA.

According to some authors Columbus discovered Guiana in 1498; others pretend the honour belongs to Vasco Nuñez, who landed on the coast of Guiana in 1504. It is likewise stated that the discovery of Guiana was accomplished by Diego de Ordas, of the kingdom of Leon, in the year 1531. He was one of the captains of Cortez in the conquest of Mexico. Sir Walter Raleigh ascended the Orinoco in 1595, and Hakluyt, the contemporary naval historian, mentions already the rivers Curitini (Corentyn), Berbice, Wapari (Abari), Maicawini (Mahaiconi), Mahawaica (Mahaica), Lemerare (Demerara), Devoritia or Dessekebe (Essequibo), Matoreeni (Mazaruni), Cuwini, (Cuyuni), Pawrooma (Pomeroon), Moruga (Morucca), Waini (Guainia), Barima, etc. as the most considerable between the Corentyn and Orinoco. The earliest accounts which we have relative to the settlement of this coast, state that in 1580 some inhabitants of Zealand, one of the provinces of the Netherlands, sent out vessels to cruize on the Amazon, and westward to the Orinoco, in quest of discoveries. They formed a settlement near the river Pomeroon, which they called Nieuw Zealand, and another at the Labari or Wapari, now Abari river, where there was an Indian village called Nibie. A settlement was afterwards effected on the west coast of the Essequibo, from which they were driven in 1596 by a party of Spaniards and Indians; they removed, therefore, further upwards in the river, and succeeded in gaining possession of a small island at the junction of the Mazaruni and Cuyuni, called Kyk-overal, from the circumstance that it afforded a view of the three rivers Cuyuni, Mazaruni, and Essequibo. In 1613 the colony of Zealanders at the banks of the Essequibo was reported to be in a flourishing condition; and eight years afterwards, namely in 1621, the government undertook to supply the colonists with negro slaves from Africa. In 1626, van Peere, who with his companions had been driven from the Orinoco, commenced to settle at the banks of the river Berbice, and cleared a considerable extent of land between the Berbice and Corentyn rivers. In 1634, thirty passengers from West Friesland arrived at the island Mecoria between the rivers Cayenne and Wya, who settled and commenced cultivating tobacco and cotton. They found here some settlers from the Netherlands, and discovered on a rising ground the ruins of a French castle, which they repaired for their own protection. The English had commenced colonization about the same time at the great Coma, now Surinam river, sixty miles up, having been expelled from the little Coma, the present Comowini, by the Caribi Indians. They rebuilt here a large Indian village called Paramaribo, which had been destroyed by the natives at their approach. This village was commanded by Captain Marshall, with about sixty settlers; but being constantly annoyed by the natives, and the climate proving unhealthy, they abandoned it afterwards.

About 1640 the French possessed themselves of the present river Surinam, and inhabited Paramaribo. The same reasons which induced the former settlers to abandon it, obliged likewise the French to leave their new colony, and to settle ultimately in Cayenne.

The English returned in 1652 to Paramaribo, and the Caribi Indians having removed from Wanica to the Coponam, they were more successful in forming a settlement.

In 1662 the whole colony was granted by Charles II. to Lord Willoughby, the then governor of Barbadoes, who named the principal river, wherein Paramaribo is situated, Surryham, in honour of the Earl of Surry; from which the whole colony took its name. The British Crown bought afterwards this colony from the heirs of Lord Willoughby, and exchanged it with the Dutch government in 1667 for New Holland, in North America, the present New York.

In 1657 the rivers Pomeroon and Morocco were settled anew by Zealanders, and the towns of New Zealand and New Middleburgh were erected on their banks.

The settlements on the Essequibo were taken in 1665 by the English, and afterwards plundered by the French, who destroyed the settlements on the Pomeroon. The same year a small English vessel of war sailed up the river Berbice, and attempted an attack of Fort Nassau, but was repulsed.

In the year 1669 the colony of Dutch Guiana, which then extended from the river Sinamari to the mouth of the Barima, which has its outflow in the Orinoco, was transferred from certain gentlemen owners in the towns of Amsterdam, Middleburgh, Flushing, and Veere, to the West India Company of Zealand.

The colony of Berbice was comprised in the charter of the West India Company; but an arrangement had been made in 1678 with the family of van Peere, of Flushing, who were the founders, and it was granted to them in perpetuity. In 1712 a French flotilla under Admiral de Casse attacked the settlement, and exacted a contribution of 300,000 florins, which was finally paid by the mercantile house of van Hoorn and Company, who received in return three fourths of the colony. In 1720 the proprietors of Berbice not having sufficient capital for the cultivation of which the colony was capable, raised a loan of 3,200,000 florins, in 1600 shares of 2000 florins each, to be employed solely in the production of sugar, cocoa, and indigo, and from the realisation of this scheme commenced the flourishing state of the colony, and a fort was built near the junction of the Canje. Coffee was introduced in 1721 from Surinam; the first export of that bean, however, is not recorded till 1752, when it amounted to a single bag.

In 1732 a constitution of Berbice was enacted by the States General; the government to be administered by a governor and council.

The colonization of Essequibo and Demerara proceeded, meanwhile, very slowly: the Company's establishment at Nibie, on the Abari, received a constitution in 1739; but we have no notice whatever of colonization having advanced to the Demerara river until 1745, when the directors of the chamber of Zealand granted permission to Andrew Pieters to lay out plantations on the uninhabited river Demerara. The title of director-general was first assumed in 1751 by the chief officer of Essequibo and Demerara, Storm van S'Gravesande, who was then commandant.

A negro insurrection in 1763 threatened the flourishing colony of Berbice with destruction; this was not subdued till eleven months after by a squadron from the Netherlands under Colonel de Salve. Six years after the woods were set on fire, as it was supposed by some rebel negroes; and the conflagration spread from the river Corentyn to the Demerara, devastating several plantations and destroying the forest.

The courts of policy and of criminal and civil justice were first established in Demerara at an island called Borselen, about twenty miles up the Demerara river; the seat of government was however removed in 1774 to the east point at the mouth of the river, and named Stabroek.

In 1711 the British fleet under Sir George Rodney took possession of all the Dutch West India colonies. Such had been the want of shipping that the quantity of produce accumulated in Demerara and Essequibo was so great that these colonies were considered the richest prizes. At the peace of 1783 the whole of these colonies were restored to Holland, when they were almost immediately after taken possession of by the French, who built forts on both shores of the river Demerara at its mouth, and compelled the planters to furnish Negro-labour. In 1785 the courts of policy of Demerara and Essequibo were united, and their meetings directed to be held at Stabroek. In 1796 the colonies surrendered to General Whyte, who with three British regiments of infantry had been sent from Barbadoes. Lieutenant Colonel Hislop was left in the government; and the troops for the most part were quartered in the Fort William Frederick, one of those fortifications which had been constructed by the French. But the officers built huts for themselves without the walls, and thus laid the foundation of that district of Georgetown which is known as Kingston. The following year (1797) a party of Spaniards attacked the post on the Morocco river, but they were repulsed with severe loss by a detachment of Dutch soldiers in British service, commanded by Captain Rochelle.

Under the protection of Great Britain, agriculture and commerce increased rapidly; and before these colonies were restored, at the peace of Amiens in 1802, to what was then called the Batavian Republic, the exports had risen to nearly 20,000 hogsheads of sugar, and about 10,000,000 pounds of coffee. They remained only for a few months in their possession, as on the breaking out of the war in 1803, Demerara and Essequibo surrendered to the British forces under General Greenfield, and Berbice to a detachment under Colonel Nicholson; since which time it has remained a British colony.

In 1812 all distinctions between the colonies of Demerara and Essequibo, whether of jurisdiction or otherwise, were abolished, the juridical establishment at Fort Island discontinued, and the courts of justice united in Demerara, and the name of Stabroek changed to Georgetown, which was declared the seat of government. The colonies Demerara and Essequibo and Berbice were finally ceded by an additional article to a convention between Great Britain and the Netherlands, signed at London on the 13th of August, to Great Britain, with the condition, that the Dutch proprietors should have liberty to trade with Holland under certain restrictions. An insurrection of the slaves on several estates on the east coast of Demerara broke out in August 1823; it was however soon quelled. Twenty of the insurgents were executed, and John Smith, of the London Missionary Society, convicted by a general court-martial of treasonable conduct in exciting the slaves to the revolt, was sentenced to death, but respited, and finally pardoned by the king, on condition of banishment from the West India colonies; he died in prison before his pardon arrived.

The foundation stone of the new public building, intended to include all the public offices, was laid in 1829 by a committee of the court of policy.

On the 21st of July, 1831, the colonies of Demerara, Essequibo, and Berbice were united into one colony, named British Guiana, and Sir Benjamin D'Urban was appointed governor and vice-admiral over the same.

Important changes have since occurred, not only in British Guiana, but in all British colonies, and the slaves received emancipation in August 1838. From this event we must commence the date of a new era, and it remains to be hoped that this so joyful change of condition in a portion of our fellow-men may be connected with blessings to them and prosperity to the colony.

II.

CAPABILITIES AND RESOURCES OF BRITISH GUIANA.

No part of the dominions under the British crown surpasses Guiana in the commdiousness of its situation for commerce, and in maritime strength, in diversity of soil and luxuriant vegetation, as conducing to national prosperity, and in the connecting the interior with the coast regions, to make these treasures available to the fullest extent. In the foregoing remarks I have given a general outline of the productions of this rich and beautiful country, and it is now my intention to state how far its capabilities and resources might prove of advantage to colonists and the mother country, and its riches be made subservient to the wants of mankind in general.

<small>Different soils of the colony.</small> The clayey and alluvial marshy land which is now under cultivation, extends to those sandy hills which I have already described, and has, when protected against the encroachment of the sea, and rendered mellow by labour, produced astonishing returns, which make it probable that if emigration to the colony increases, its produce will be doubled in every ten years. This extensive district is at present only partly cultivated with sugar, coffee and cotton, the three staple articles of the colony, intermixed with a few plantains. To enable my readers to judge of the richness and fertility of that soil, I may observe that

it has been recorded to have produced 6000 lbs. of sugar on an acre, or 20,000 lbs. of plantains*. To this fertility the former prosperity of the colony was to be ascribed; how much that prosperity might be increased, if the flow of emigration were to be directed to British Guiana, may be imagined chiefly, if many of its indigenous productions, which, comparatively speaking, are almost unknown, were added to the list of exports or internal consumption. It wants only the means of drawing them from their obscurity, to open new resources to the enterprising emigrant.

It is not probable that British Guiana contains gold and silver mines. I have explored its chief rivers, and have visited the mountains which traverse the heart of the colony, without finding the slightest indication of precious metals. The bare and rugged mountains of Pacaraima, and the chain which takes the direction of the meridian in the equatorial regions, are the most likely to possess in their bowels gold and silver; but the colony possesses a treasure superior to those metals, and able to enrich millions of its inhabitants, namely, its amazing fertility, and the diversity of its soil and natural productions.

Savannahs adapted for grazing grounds. The sand-hills are followed by savannahs, which generally extend to the first rocky belt, and are sometimes interspersed with woods and rivulets. They are most extensive between the rivers Demerara and Berbice; they are also frequent between the latter river and the Corentyn; but these must not be confused with those of the Rupununi, which are sterile. The former are clothed with nutritious

* I have been informed that at the estate, Mary's Hope, on the Corentyn, 8000lbs. of sugar have been produced on an acre; and with regard to plantains it is generally calculated that an acre gives seven bunches a week throughout the year. The above weight of 20,000lbs. is by no means extraordinary, since instances are known that 30,000lbs. of plantains have been produced.

and wholesome grasses, and in consequence of the number of springs and brooks, and the thickets of wood with which they are interspersed, it appears as if Nature herself had pointed them out for the pasture-ground of thousands of cattle and horses. Those between the rivers Berbice and Demerara occupy upwards of three thousand square miles, and the favourable circumstance that they are plentifully watered by tributaries of the Demerara and Berbice, and interrupted by wood-land to afford shade during the heat of the day, enhances their value as grazing-grounds.

<small>Soil adapted to the cultivation of the vine, the olive, and coffee.</small>

The soil between these hills and the central ridge of mountains, consists of a strong fertile loam, mixed with clay and vegetable mould, and sometimes with ferruginous matter, which gives it a reddish appearance. Indeed it is a rich primitive soil, retentive and springy. The fitness of the hilly tract, or central chain of mountains for the cultivation of coffee, and in consequence of its gravelly and clayey nature for the cultivation of the vine and olive, is perfect. The springy soil in these mountains and valleys would produce almost anything; but the sides of the mountains, I am sure, as far as my experience goes, are qualified for the production of the finest grapes, equal to those of Madeira, and without much labour or expense; these fertile regions have a great advantage over the African Isles, in not being subject to great droughts. The Catholic missionaries, who before the struggle for independence broke out in the former Spanish colonies, were settled on the banks of the rivers Caroni and Caura, tributaries to the Orinoco, are known to have cultivated the vine. The revolutionary war destroyed their missions, deprived them of their lives, or rendered them fugitives.

<small>Soil for the</small>

In ascending the river Berbice, and having passed the

central ridge of mountains, we found, in lat. 4° 20′ N., the bank of the river low, and forming large inlets. The understratum of the soil was here highly retentive, while on the surface it consisted of a clayey marl, mixed with mud and sand, the deposit of periodical floodings of the river; it is therefore particularly qualified for the cultivation of rice; and thousands of square acres, now lying in a worse than useless state, might thus become subservient to the wants of man. This morasty soil is bordered by gently undulating ground of great fecundity. The soil which I found between the two rivers, when crossing from the Berbice to the Essequibo, was very rich: we found near the banks of the Essequibo, at the abandoned Indian settlement Primoss, numerous cocoa-trees; they extended more than a mile from the river's banks, being loaded with fruits in different stages. Though some of the trees might have been planted by the Indians, it was evident that nature had assisted in propagating them: their luxuriant growth and numerous fruit proved that htey throve well in this soil.*

extensive cultivation of rice and cocoa.

The vegetation of the river Rupununi is far less luxuriant. The savannah which approaches its banks, consists of arid sands upon a clay substratum, and are unproductive. Woods form only here and there a fringe along the rivers, and either disappear entirely at some distance from the banks, or become quite stunted in growth: the only fertile soil at the regions of the savannahs is along the foot of mountains, or on their ridges.

If we turn our attention to the consideration, how far the mineralogical productions of Guiana might be rendered useful to economical purposes, the clays of the alluvial flats first claim our attention, as being nearest to

Clays fit for the manufacture of earthenware and bricks.

---

* The cocoa-tree is found indigenous on the banks of the Rio Branco; it is therefore more than probable that those at Primoss are likewise indigenous.

the cultivated part of the colony. The immense masses of fine white clay of the river Corentyn would probably prove a valuable article for the manufacture of stoneware or porcelain, while the coloured and coarser clay might be used in the manufacture of bricks, which, at present, for the construction of the necessary buildings on sugar-estates, are imported at great expense from Europe. The Indians are the only individuals who prepare a coarse earthenware by mere manual labour from the clays of the country; the white clays of the Corentyn alternate with quartz particles and layers of sand, the latter a necessary ingredient in the fabrication of porcelain. The sand which forms the first elevation, when penetrating from the sea-coast towards the interior, contains much silex, and is well adapted for the manufacture of glass. Experiments were made with it in Boston, U. S., which proved highly satisfactory, and produced a better glassware than is generally manufactured from the sands in the United States. These cliffs become of further interest, as their structure, if judged of by analogy, renders it probable that coal might be found in that situation: if such proved the fact, it would add a new and valuable resource to those which the colony already possesses.

Sand for the manufacture of glass.

Steam is not only employed in the manufacture of sugar, but likewise in cleaning the coffee of its husks and the cotton of its seeds. Coal is at present imported from the mother country, comparatively at an easy freight: but would this continue if Great Britain should be involved in a war with any other power? Setting aside all other advantages which it offers, a reference to this circumstance is alone sufficient to demonstrate the vital importance of the discovery of coal measures in British Guiana.

Guiana is not likely to possess mineral riches.

Though it may be possible that gold and silver mines exist in the mountain chain of Pacaraima, no native specimens have ever been brought by the Indians to the colony, although they frequently bring the mountain crystals, red chalcedony, and coloured agates. Captain Cordiero, then commandant of Fort San Joaquim on the Brazilian frontier, told me in 1835 that the Indians from the upper river Branco had brought him at different times specimens of native silver.

The Dutch made several attempts at mining in 1721, and sent a miner by the name of Hildebrand to examine the interior; but though his search was conducted with great attention, he did not discover any indications of the precious metals. Red iron ore is sometimes met with in the granite regions; but the brown iron ore is most conspicuous in the tracts previously alluded to. I have observed, elsewhere, that the oxide of manganese, which I have seen in the possession of the Indians, consisted only of small quantities. Whether large mines of that metal are extant in Guiana it is difficult to say, and the limited use of it does not increase the importance of such a discovery. The Indians employ it to give a lustre to their native pottery. *Iron ore, oxide of manganese.*

The granitic tract in the vicinity of the mouth of the Mazaruni, and the adjacent country, has already afforded building-materials, and has been used in the construction of wharfs and in the building of houses: if once fairly introduced, it will be of great advantage to the colony. The tracts of sandstones in the river Corentyn may prove likewise useful; some of the blocks would square ten to twelve feet. *Building-stone.*

The vegetation of the interior contains treasures which need only be developed to insure the welfare of millions, and to minister to the comforts, necessaries and elegancies of mankind in general. The beautiful timber which abounds in the vast forests, and covers millions of acres, profits, under present circumstances, only a few; *Fitness of indigenous timber trees for naval architecture.*

and if we except the timber which is employed for colonial use, scarcely more than one hundred to one hundred and fifty pieces have been exported annually. This trifling export does not arise in consequence of the inferior quality of the timber; and, as every competent judge acknowledges, the mora and green-heart* vie or even surpass the East India teak and African oak; but the high rate of labour, and the trouble connected at present with transporting the timber from the far interior to the coast, allows only a trifling profit to the enterprising wood-cutter. There are about one thousand eight hundred to two thousand individuals employed in that trade, of which number seven-tenths are Indians, the remainder are Blacks and Coloured people, with but a few Whites.

It is well known that vessels built with indigenous wood (and there are now two in the trade of Demerara, the Mountaineer and the Christina, which are built entirely of timbers furnished from Guiana,) are of superior description with regard to strength and durability: the vessels employed immediately in the colony are in a great measure constructed of indigenous woods.

Proposal for establishing a naval arsenal or dockyard in Demerara.

If the great expense connected with supplying the British navy with timber from North America, Italy, and the Baltic be duly considered, it becomes an object of consideration whether it would not be advantageous to establish a naval arsenal in Demerara. The river is navigable for vessels of one hundred and fifty to two hundred tons for one hundred miles up; and though the bar does not allow vessels that draw more than twenty

* Several cargoes of greenheart have been sent to the Clyde, where it is preferred to any other timber; but the want of labourers in Guiana makes it impossible to meet the demand. Another cargo was lately imported at Liverpool and bought by the corporation at a shilling per foot higher than any other wood.

feet of water to go over it even at spring tides, it affords a safe and commodious harbour for thousands of that description, where they may anchor in five to ten fathoms water; indeed, the river from Fort Point to Hababu Creek may be said to form one vast harbour. Here the ships lie undisturbed by gales and hurricanes, which are unknown phænomena; thus its fitness for a naval arsenal becomes evident.

I have already alluded to the valuable mora, (*Mora excelsa*, Benth.), one of the trees most abundant in the forest. The wood is very durable in any situation in and out of the water, remarkably strong, tough, and not liable to split. Its crooked timbers would be of the greatest utility for knees; and the finest stems for vessels of any size might be procured, as well as the choice and valuable pieces in request for keels, kelsons, stern-posts, floors, beams, &c. The close nature of its wood, which never splits, recommends it for bulwarks of men-of-war, bomb-vessels and gun-boats. Not less recommendable are the planks of green-heart: siruabally for planking; the purple-heart for bulwarks, gun-carriages, mortar-beds, &c.; and the red cedar, which reaches a height of upwards of eighty feet, for masts and spars of vessels. The colony is also rich in woods which are adapted for cabinet-work, turnery, and ornamental purposes, many of which are at present entirely unknown to the cabinet-makers of Europe, and which only in a few houses of the opulent colonists have been used for furnishing their rooms. The elegant appearance of these woods in a great measure hides the want of taste in the execution of the furniture. Pre-eminent among these ornamental woods stands the beautiful letterwood, which in elegance of appearance, and the readiness with which it takes polish, recommends it above all others to notice.

[Side note: The Mora tree, Green-heart, Siruabally, &c. peculiarly adapted for naval architecture, cabinet-work, &c.]

If it should please Her Majesty's Government to encourage the timber-trade, it would not only open a new resource to the Government, but afford double advantage to the colony. In consequence of the increased demand, the lands would be cleared, and by this a great step towards civilization and an improvement in the health of the colony would be gained.

Among the British possessions in South America, Honduras takes a great share in the export of timbers; and though British Guiana neither possesses the logwood nor the mahogany, it possesses other timber-trees and dyes equally useful; while Guiana has the advantage, that it may be approached with less danger to the navigator than Honduras, and is never subjected to hurricanes.

<small>Medicinal plants.</small> In the foregoing remarks I have endeavoured to make the reader acquainted with some of the trees which, with reference to their timber, are of importance to commerce. Of equal, if not greater value, are the trees and plants from which medicinal substances may be obtained, and which, at present unheeded and unsought for by the colonists, do not profit mankind, and may be considered buried riches. It would be in vain to attempt a description of all the medicinal plants with which the dense forest of the interior abounds. I shall therefore satisfy myself with enumerating the most remarkable.

<small>Laurel oil.</small> Trees which belong to the Laurel tribe are very numerous in Guiana, and are not only important for their aromatic and stomachic qualities, but likewise for the volatile oil which is obtained merely by making incisions in the bark; this oil is used in rheumatic complaints, or in general externally as a discutient, and internally as a diuretic and diaphoretic. It commands in the colony a price of ten guilders (14s.) per quart; several quarts may be obtained by a single incision.

The bark of *Laurus Cinnamomoides* is warm and aromatic. The Mabaima or Amabaima of the natives, or *Casca preciosa* of the Brazilians, is a sweet, aromatic bark which comes from a tree that belongs likewise to the Laurel family. I have no doubt that the tree which furnishes the Sassafras nuts of the London shops (*Laurus Pucheri*) will be found indigenous in Guiana. — Wild cinnamon.

The forests of Guiana produce plants which possess powerful febrifugal properties. On the banks which border the river Berbice in the fourth and fifth parallel, the *Quassia amara*, or bitter ash, and further south, the *Portlandia hexandra*, are to be obtained in abundance. Several of the *Anonaceæ*, as *Uvaria febrifuga* (*Frutta de Burro* of the Colombians), are used as a febrifuge. The Indians of the Rupununi set a great value on the bark of a tree which they call Allissau; in the absence of its flowers I considered it to belong to the Bucku tribe (*Diosmæ*). The *Simaruba, Tachia guianensis, Malpighia febrifuga*, and numerous others, would prove useful for their febrifugal properties. — Trees and plants which possess febrifugal properties.

The violet tribe comprises a plant which furnishes the Ipecacuanha, namely *Ionidium parviflorum*. The root of the *Cephaelis Ipecacuanha*, found in the damp and shaded forests of the interior, furnishes the best Ipecacuanha. A small creeping plant, a species of *Vandellia*, is used as an emetic by the Indians with great success. — Ipecacuanha.

The diuretic and demulcent powers of the Sarsaparilla are well known; and the Sarsa de Rio Negro is most esteemed for that purpose. Guiana possesses several kinds, and the *Duroquaro*, one of the indigenous species, is used with great effect by the Indians. If the *Smilax siphilitica*, which is considered to furnish the best sarsaparilla, should not be found, it might be cultivated with — Sarsaparilla.

success in British Guiana. The root of the *Phiolacca decandra, Helicteris Sacarolha, Waltheria Douradinha,* are used in siphilitic diseases.

Caoutchouc.

That valuable substance Caoutchouc is yielded by divers trees and plants, viz. a species of fig-tree, several of the family of *Euphorbiaceæ*, and the hya-hya or milk-tree, which affords a milky secretion, possessing a small quantity of caoutchouc, and has been used as a substitute for milk.

Balsam of copaiva, umiri, elemi, acouchi, gum anime, gum lac.

Many trees of the forests of Guiana are famed for their fragrant resinous juice and healing qualities. The balsam copaiva is yielded by the genus *Copaifera*, of which there are divers species in Guiana. I have met frequently in the Canucu mountains the species which is said to yield that substance in the greatest abundance. The *Icica Carana* produces a substance like gum elemi, the *Icica acouchini* the balsam of acouchi, the *Humirium floribundum* the balsam of umiri, the *Amyris ambrosiaca*, an immense tree, the fragrant resin of conima. The latter tree, called *Haiowa* or *Sepou* by the Indians, is most abundant. The Tonko bean is very fragrant, and possesses a volatile oil, which contains a peculiar principle called coumarin. Several species of *Anoniaceæ* yield likewise a fragrant gum, highly prized by the Indians, and from their flowers essential oils might be extracted. The locust-tree, or *Hymenæa*, furnishes the gum anime. It is found in abundance, and might be used as gum lac. Several species of *Garcinia* as well as *Clusia* possess gamboge.

Vegetable tallow.

The Dali, a species of *Myristica*, a large and majestic tree, is very frequent along the banks of rivers; its seeds when immersed in boiling water furnish a vegetable tallow, which has been used with effect for the preparation of candles by several colonists.

Most prominent among the vegetable oils is that pressed out of the nut of the crab-wood tree (*Carapa Guianensis*); it is used in the colony for burning, but at present small quantities are only manufactured by Indians, who anoint their hair with it, and the strength and fine gloss which distinguish it is ascribed to the use of that oil. They press likewise a sweet oil from the fruits of certain palm trees, chiefly from the *Acuyuru* (*Astrocaryon aculeatum*), and Cucurit palm (*Maxiliana regia*).

Vegetable oils.

The number of woods which furnish valuable dyes is considerable. I allude to the Brazil wood, the fustic-tree, the black dye of the *Lana* (*Genipa americana*) and *Serada*, the red dye of the *Maparakuni erythroxylum*, different *Malpighidæ*, and the useful dye Arnatto or Roucou, which is indigenous, and thrives without care*. The *Bignonia chica* affords a dye similar to the *Arnatto*. The plant possesses it in such abundance, that it exudes like resin when the wood is wounded; it dyes a bright orange. To the same family belongs the Manariballi (*Jacaranda ovali-* and *acuti-folia*), which affords an excellent remedy against that dreadful disease, the yaws; a decoction of its leaves is given to the patient inwardly, and he is likewise directed to wash his body in it.

Dyes.

Guiana possesses several trees, the bark of which affords the principle of tanning. The bark of the *Avicennia tomentosa*, and a species of *Malpighia*, which is abundant on the savannahs in the interior, is much used by the Bra-

Tanners' bark.

---

* It will scarcely be believed, that the *Arnatto*, which is so extensively used for colouring, is at present imported from France, viâ New York, to avoid, like the slave-grown coffees, the foreign duty. It is an indigenous plant in Guiana; the banks of the Upper Corentyn are covered with it, but there are not sufficient people to render the natural productions of the colony of use.

zilians for that purpose. The heart of the mora tree is considered as valuable for tanning as oak.

Fruits.

There are many fruits grateful to the palate, and wholesome withal, which are the productions of the forests. Among a great number, I mention only the Pine-apple, the Guava, the Marmalade fruit, the delicious fruits of the Anona tribe, the Sapodilla, several species of Passiflora, the Brazil and Suwarrow or Souari nuts; the latter, which are the fruits of *Cariocar tomentosum*, and various others of the same genus, may be considered as some of the most delicious of the nut kind, and would furnish a sweet and bland oil.

Ropes, cordage, &c.

The leaves of some of the *Bromeliæ* which grow on the arid savannahs, furnish a fibre, of which the natives make thread and ropes: it is uncommonly strong and durable. The fibres of the *Agave vivipara* have been used for the same purpose, and those of the young leaves of the Ita palm (*Mauritia flexuosa*) are woven into hammocks, ropes, and baskets, by the Warrau and Arawaak Indians: these ropes do not, as at present manufactured, sustain long exposure or damp situations. The cultivation of the Piazaba palm (*Attalea funifera*) might prove of great importance. This palm is indigenous on the Rio Negro and the Cassiquiare; and of its petioles a cordage is manufactured, which is extremely light, and floats upon the water, and is more durable in the navigation of rivers than ropes of hemp. It is extensively used in the Brazilian navy, and large quantities are exported to Para, and to many of the West India islands.

Resources of the Colony, its staple Productions; and Proposals for making the large tracts of fertile land available which lie perfectly waste in the interior.

The productiveness of the soil is so great, that the Indian bestows but little labour on the cultivation of his provision-field. He plants cassada, maize, plantains, sweet potatoes, yams, &c., and leaves it to nature to ripen them. The soil, which is generally selected on the foot or side of mountains, and which it costs him comparatively little trouble to put in order, yields abundant returns for the remainder of the year. I sent samples of cassada root, yams, and Indian corn, cultivated at the foot of the Pacaraima chain, in 1836, to Georgetown; and these productions were acknowledged to surpass in size and quality those produced at the coast regions. *[marginal note: Indian provision-grounds: their productiveness a proof of the fertility of the soil.]*

The bunches of plantains which I saw at the Canucu mountains, at a height of 3000 feet above the level of the sea, might have vied with the largest from the fertile island Puerto Rico. It is generally believed on the coast, that this plant succeeds only in a 'pegass soil': the plantain is, however, with the Macusis and Wapisianas, one of the necessaries of life, and thrives equally well, if not better, on the clayey and gravely soil of these regions: this refers likewise to the banana or bacouva.

The staples of the colony are at present sugar, coffee, and cotton. It would be useless to dwell upon the importance of the cultivation of the first article, which has been the foundation of the prosperity of the colony. Although coffee and cotton were formerly almost solely cultivated, these productions are now in a great measure neglected, and the preference is given to the cultivation of the sugar-cane. The coast-regions only have hitherto *[marginal note: Staple commodities: sugar, coffee and cotton.]*

been cultivated for the production of sugar; but that many tracts in the interior are equally qualified for it, is proved by the immense size of the canes I have met with in different parts of the interior, some of which measured six to seven inches in circumference, though they were produced on a mountain between 2300 and 2500 feet above the plain, without any weeding or attention. I saw a quantity of sugar-cane at an abandoned Caribbee settlement, called Mourre Mourre Patee, on the river Essequibo, which, left to nature, produced as fine canes as ever I met with on the coast.

Coffee was for a length of time almost the only staple of Berbice and Demerara; it has since been much neglected, the cultivation of sugar being substituted for it. Its use throughout the civilized world has so much increased, that its importation has been trebled the last ten years, and is now estimated at 20,000 tons. The consumption in the United Kingdom amounted in 1831 to 9865 tons, or upwards of twenty-two millions of pounds. Its cultivation must therefore be an object of great interest to the colony. At present it is restricted to the coast regions, where the soil is very rich, and the trees are often luxuriant without ensuring fruit of a good quality: the most favourable situation is undoubtedly the side of a hill, where the soil is springy. There is, perhaps, in British Guiana, no tract better qualified for the cultivation of that bean, than the central ridge of mountains. If an increased population should permit the interior to be cultivated, this tract would produce coffee equal in quality to that from Jamaica and Martinique, which is considered the best in the West Indies, and would soon surpass Jamaica in quantity of export, though it is estimated at 20,000,000 pounds. The outlay of capital for the establishment of a coffee plantation being small, this circumstance would offer greater inducements to settlers; and if in the selection of the soil and situation some care were bestowed, I see no reason why it should not equal the Mocha bean.

The indigenous cottons are very numerous; and the Indian has generally a few shrubs of that useful plant around his hut: however, I have seen the industrious Macusi cultivating it more extensively. The hammocks which the Indians manufacture of it, are valued for their strength and durability, and are considered superior to the European article. Like the staples before enumerated, cotton has been only cultivated by the colonists at the coast regions; but its cultivation has in a great measure been abandoned, because our cottons, raised by free labour and in a British colony, were undersold by those produced by slaves in the United States.

Cotton: the excellent quality of the indigenous cottons in the interior.

If, with regard to the abundance and cheapness of labour, British Guiana were put on the same footing as the slave states in America, an inexhaustible supply of cotton of every description might be produced. There is no doubt, that all kinds of cotton, from the best long staple down to the finest short staple, might be cultivated in the colony, as the kind which does not thrive in one soil or climate might be produced in another. An extent of sea-coast of two hundred and eighty miles from the river Corentyn to the mouth of the Orinoko, would produce cotton vieing with the best in the world.

I doubt the opinion that the finest cotton will not grow at a greater distance than twenty miles from the sea. I have sent samples of the wild cotton from the interior to the colony, which were admired by competent judges for their fine long staple and silky appearance. No care whatever had been bestowed upon the cultivation of these plants, which grew at a distance of three or four hundred miles from the coast. Although the growth of the plant was not luxuriant, it was covered abundantly with cotton of most excellent quality; indeed it would be highly advisable to the cotton-growers at the coast to exchange the seeds.

Vegetable Productions, which, although they do not as yet form articles of export or internal consumption, might be raised with advantage by emigrants who are not in possession of large capital.

Sugar, coffee, and cotton are the commodities which have been hitherto almost the only objects of cultivation in Guiana; but it must not thence be inferred that other articles are properly excluded. The fertility of the soil promises a safe return for the investment of capital in the cultivation of other crops, which would open new resources to the colony. If the stream of emigration, which has been directed to other and more distant colonies, should flow towards British Guiana, and the great disparity between the land to be cultivated and the want of labourers to cultivate it be removed, would not the enterprising farmer, who knew that his capital was not sufficient to embark in the expensive cultivation of the sugar-cane, select some other product, from which he might expect to receive an adequate return for the labour required and the capital employed? The altered circumstances of the labouring population will produce a new æra in colonial history; and while formerly the cultivation of sugar engrossed the mind of the speculator, on which he hazarded frequently not only his own means, but likewise the property of others, the altered state of things will produce a vast change in agriculture; a new class of cultivators will arise, who perhaps may be compared to the farmers of the mother country. The vast establishments now existing will be broken up into separate concerns of more manageable dimensions: the different occupations of agriculturist, miller, and distiller will no longer be combined, but, as in the mother country, each individual will follow that branch of industry, to which the nature of his property (if he possess any) or of his abilities (if he does not) may direct him. The lands are adapted for numerous other branches of agriculture, and among them the less wealthy cultivator will make his choice. New excitement to commercial enterprize will thus be raised, and additional prosperity may naturally be expected to follow. I have already pointed out, that among the vegetable productions of Guiana, a great many are objects of desire in Europe: their number might be considerably increased; and I venture to propose such as I know might be successfully cultivated, from my researches in the interior of British Guiana.

The cultivation of rice would prove a very productive branch of husbandry; and as it has formed of late years a principal article of food for the labouring population, it is of great importance that it should be cultivated in sufficient quantities, if not for export, by all means for the internal demand of the colony, which does not employ the resources which she possesses to produce food for her inhabitants. The all-engrossing object, the cultivation of sugar, has for several years usurped thousands of acres which were formerly dedicated to the production of plantains, once the chief food of the labourer. The land on the coast is no doubt well adapted for the production of rice; but we will not encroach upon the soil at present planted with sugar-cane. There is a tract be-

Rice.

tween the rivers Berbice and Essequibo, in 4° 20' N. latitude, which nature itself appears to have designed for the growth of that article. It possesses the means of constant irrigation, and at the first subsiding of the periodical inundations, when the soil is left like soft mud, the seeds might be put in. The banks of the river Berbice are here so low, that irrigation might be easily procured even in times of great drought. I am fully persuaded in my mind that two crops of rice might be procured annually; indeed it is on record, that a Mr. Bielstein, who cultivated this article on a small scale at the lower Essequibo, raised repeatedly three crops in a year. The cultivation of rice would thus cover thousands of acres which are at present a perfect wilderness; and food for the lower classes would be provided, which at present is mostly imported from a foreign country, which, perhaps, at an earlier or later date may be at issue with Great Britain, beside that the rice procured from the United States is raised by slave labour.

Indian corn, or maize. Of the Cereal grains, the Indian corn deserves more attention than it has hitherto received. The maize is indigenous; and that the coast does by no means afford the best soil for its cultivation, is proved by the superiority of the maize raised by the Indians in the interior. It is cultivated as the principal crop in Egypt, and to a large extent in the United States, chiefly in the southern slave states, whence it is imported into British Guiana.

Millet. Indian millet, which under the name of Guinea corn, is so extensively cultivated in the West Indies, might be raised to a large extent. I think it constitutes in the Bahamas the principal article for the nourishment of the labouring classes. But of the greatest import will prove

Victoria wheat. the introduction of the Victoria wheat into our West Indian and South American colonies; and there is every probability that its cultivation will be attended with success. It is said to grow equally well in arid plains as in humid mountains, and it promises three crops annually. This grain is likely to afford therefore new resources of those fertile regions, and will tend to make the colony less dependent upon foreign imports: the sudden and often enormous rise of that necessary article flour, in British Guiana, when the import is not adequate to the consumption, proves on what precarious footing the maintenance of the inhabitants is placed. The Victoria wheat has succeeded in Barbadoes and Jamaica, islands which cannot vie in fertility and diversity of soil with Guiana. Indeed we have reason to hope, that with sufficient labour, a quantity equal to that raised about Calcutta might be produced in Guiana. If the dearth and famine be considered, which at present is raging in New South Wales and Van Diemen's Land, it becomes almost the sacred duty of the legislative body to encourage by all means in their power the introduction and extensive cultivation of this Cereal grain, to prevent a similar calamity, which, thanks to the Almighty and the fertility of the soil, has been hitherto unknown in British Guiana.

The only English colonies where that nutritious and wholesome substance, cocoa, is cultivated, are Trinidad, Grenada, and St. Vincent: in Jamaica and Guiana it has given place to the production of sugar; and though it forms such an important article in the import of the United Kingdom, the quantity introduced from British plantations is but trifling. The cocoa tree delights in a rich and springy soil, or in which irrigation may be admitted. While we crossed from the river Berbice, to the Essequibo, we met a number of choco-

<small>Cocoa.</small>

late-nut trees, near the abandoned Caribi settlement of Primoss. It is not to be doubted that the trees were originally planted by the Indians; but from their number and the distance from the river, I judged they were propagated by nature: though they were overshaded by larger trees, and had for many years been neglected, they had reached nevertheless a height of from thirty to forty feet, and the luxuriant growth and the abundance of fruit proved that the plant was satisfied with the soil. The forests at the banks of the Rio Branco, in the vicinity of Santa Maria and Carmo, abound in wild cocoa trees, the fruits of which are collected by the scanty population of that district for their own use. The cultivation of cocoa will be most suitable to the less wealthy individual, as it demands so little labour and outlay. M. de Humboldt observes, in alluding to Spanish America, that cocoa plantations are occupied by persons of humble condition, who prepare for themselves and their children a slow but certain fortune; a single labourer is sufficient to aid them in their plantations, and thirty thousand trees, once established, assure competence for a generation and a half.

Vanilla. Different species of vanilla are natives of Guiana; and it is found in large quantities along the banks of its rivers, and in the wooded districts which intersperse the savannahs. It is well known that it is added to chocolate to give it an aromatic flavour, but it is likewise used for several other purposes in confectionary; and the oily and balsamic substance which the minute seeds possess may be found to have medicinal qualities. Its cultivation can be connected with no difficulties; it needs only to plant the slips among trees, and to keep them clear of weeds. It would prove therefore a great addition to a cocoa plantation. In 1825 the price was in Germany sixty rix-dollars (equal to nine pounds) per pound, and twenty-five to thirty dollars are paid for it in Martinique.

Tobacco is considered indigenous in South America, whence it is said to have found its way to Virginia, from which place it was introduced by Sir Walter Raleigh. Though it cannot be considered a necessary of life, its use is so extensive, that it forms a considerable item in the revenue of nations, and its successful cultivation is therefore of importance. With the exception of the Macuba tobacco, which is cultivated in Martinique in a peculiar soil, the tobacco of Cuba is considered the finest in the world. The sample of tobacco which I sent from the interior of British Guiana to the commercial rooms in Georgetown, was pronounced to be equal in quality to the Havannah, and even to surpass it, in consequence of its thinner ribs; indeed it was observed by an able judge, that tobacco of equal quality had never been imported in Guiana.

Tobacco.

At every Indian settlement some tobacco-plants are found to be cultivated at their provision-fields; but when once planted, no further attention is paid to it, and the leaf is cured in the most simple manner, by being hung up in the Indian's hut; it possesses nevertheless, what a connoisseur would call high flavour and aromatic qualities: how much more might its excellence be increased by proper attention being paid to its cultivation!

The cinnamon tree, though not indigenous, has been successfully cultivated in the Isle of Bourbon and the Mauritius, and it is now naturalized in those isles. It was introduced into Guiana in 1772, and there are a few planters who have several specimens of that aromatic tree in their gardens: however, it has never become an object of export. The healthy state of the trees and their luxuriant

Cinnamon, nutmegs, and other spices.

growth would ensure its becoming an article of commerce. The surface of the land where it is cultivated in Ceylon, is a pure white sand, under which is a deep stratum of rich mould. The extensive tracts south of the sandy ridges present the same soil in British Guiana. We are told that from twenty-five to twenty-six thousand people are employed in Ceylon in the cultivation of the cinnamon-tree, and the preparation of its bark for commerce. I have already observed that a wild kind of cinnamon is indigenous in Guiana, the bark of which is used as a simple by the natives.

Of equal interest would prove the cultivation of the nutmeg. Trials have been made in Trinidad; and samples having been submitted to the society for the encouragement of arts, they pronounced them equal to the eastern produce, and awarded their gold medal to the successful cultivator. The principal supply of nutmegs is at present imported from the East; but to prove the importance of the cultivation of the nutmeg-tree, I observe that the average home consumption is estimated at ten thousand pounds every month, or one hundred and twenty thousand pounds per annum. Guiana possesses an indigenous species of the nutmeg-tree; however, its fruits are small and very pungent, and cannot be used as a spice.

Pepper and pimento. Pepper has been cultivated with great success in Cayenne, and it forms already an article of export. The rich soil in mountains, valleys, or along the banks of rivers which are not subjected to inundations, is considered to be the most eligible: the plant is trailed against other trees, and might be raised in company with nutmeg-and cinnamon-trees.

The pepper-plant bears abundantly, and in Sumatra a full-grown vine has been known to produce six to seven pounds; the average produce of one thousand vines is however stated to produce only about four hundred and fifty pounds. The pimento, or allspice, is a native of South America, and would have become undoubtedly an article of high interest if the spices of the eastern hemisphere had not been previously introduced. In Jamaica it thrives where nothing else would grow: if Guiana should enter therefore into the cultivation of spice, a favourite situation for that tree might be easily found on the banks of the Rupununi.

The ginger cultivated in the West Indies is considered superior to that of the East, but it is of less importance to commerce. Ginger.

The cardamoms are a production of a plant of the same tribe as the ginger, and might be cultivated with that aromatic root as well as the turmeric or curcuma; the latter of which is not only esteemed for aromatic and stimulating properties, but likewise as a dye. Cardamoms an turmeric

The indigo imported from the western hemisphere was for some time considered superior in quality to that of the East. Its cultivation however has been neglected, and the Bengal indigo is preferred at present to any imported from South America, where it is only cultivated by the Brazilians and Colombians. If proper attention were paid to the cultivation of the plant, and to the preparation of the dye, it is very likely part of that important trade would be brought back. It thrives best in a moist climate; and the interior of Guiana, chiefly newly cleared land, would be well adapted for it. Indigo.

Numerous other articles might be recommended to be cultivated, which at present are entirely overlooked; among these is the plant that furnishes the opium, which, for English consumption, is imported from Turkey; senna, and numerous species of cassia to which genus that drug belongs, are indigenous to Guiana; sarsaparilla, cinchona, or Peruvian bark, &c.; for all of which the colony would afford a proper soil for cultivation. To these medicinal plants we may add the grape-vine, figs, olives (which have been already cultivated with success by the missionaries at the iver Carony, before the internal struggles of Colombia commenced): the cochineal insect and silk-worm would offer another addition. Our relations with China are at present on a critical footing. I need not dwell on the vast importance of the tea-trade, which is so closely connected with the decision of the pending misunderstanding. The cultivation of the tea-plant has been tried at Trinidad, and would have been successful, if the all-engrossing cultivation of sugar had not prevented it. Guiana possesses the soil of Trinidad, and tea might be raised there.

Fisheries. The rivers of Guiana are at certain seasons stocked with fish; and during that period parties of men proceed from the lower Essequibo to the falls, in order to procure the fish called pacou, which are caught in large numbers, slightly salted, and dried on the rocks.

But of greater importance than the pacou, is the existence of one of the largest freshwater fishes in the Rupununi, namely the Arapaima, or Pirarucu, which attains occasionally a length of twelve feet, and weighs upwards of three hundred pounds. It is used fresh and salted, and affords the means of subsistence to a large number of inhabitants on the river Negro and the Amazon. Were the fishing-ground on the Rupununi attended to during the dry season, an abundance of fish might be obtained for internal consumption and occasional traffic with the coast. Of other delicious fish, I mention the Laulau, which reaches nearly the size of the Arapaima, the Gillbagre, Lucanani, Haimara, Cartabac, Paiara, Bashaw, and many others, which in delicacy vie with our most esteemed European fish. Fishing is entirely neglected, and the immense numbers and great variety of the finny tribe profit but few. When the rivers begin to rise, the fish retire toward the heads of brooks, and a great many vegetable substances being swept from the land by the torrents of rain, they find sufficient nourishment, and do not bite. Game, chiefly deer, is sometimes abundant at the upper savannahs. While travelling over those which skirt the Pacaraima mountains, we procured sometimes, in the course of a few hours, from four to five deer. The maipuri, or tapir, frequents the forests along marshes and rivers: its flesh resembles beef, and is much liked by the Indians. Two species of wild hog, the acouri or agouti, the delicious cuba or paca, the waterhaas or capybara, and many others, administer to the wants of man, or form delicacies.

Numerous is the feathered game, resembling in appearance, or by their luxuriant eating, our European game-birds. Among the most famed I mention the powis, or wild turkey, the hannaqua or Guiana pheasant, the dauraqua or partridge, the anamo, the curri-curri or curlew, the Orinoco goose or wanama, and a great variety of wild ducks, among which is an indigenous Muscovi duck. It is however my opinion, that the animal creation of Guiana cannot offer any articles of commerce, if we except the few deer-skins, and those of the water dog or Guiana otter, which have been declared by hatters to be equal to the best beaver-skins. It is, however, far different with the herds of wild cattle and horses which graze on the vast savannahs of the Pacaraima mountains, and which, with very little exception, have hitherto afforded food only to beasts of prey. The superstition of the Indians does not allow them to eat the meat of cattle, and

Feathered game.

Wild cattle.

the few Brazilians who live in the neighbourhood of the Fortalezza of São Joaquim need but few for their subsistence; they are killed more for the value of their hides. These cattle descend from some Brazilian government farms, which were established towards the end of the last century by brigadier Manoel de Gama: three of these farms are in the vicinity of fort São Joaquim, at the confluence of the Tacutu with the Rio Branco, and two more further east. During the struggle of the revolution they were neglected, and the two at some distance from the fort were entirely abandoned, and the cattle dispersed over the savannahs, where they have multiplied. When I crossed the savannahs of the river Mahu, I met frequently herds of thirty to fifty; and Captain Cordiero, then commandant of fort São Joaquim, assured me that many thousands were grazing on the banks of the Tacutu and Rio Branco. The number which are still at the imperial farms in the vicinity of the Fortalezza he told me amounted to about three thousand, which are regularly tended by herdsmen, and their number is kept up. The meat of those which are slaughtered is salted and dried, and sent with the hides every three or four months to Barra (or Manaos).

It has been ascertained to the full satisfaction of several eminent physicians, that the sickness and mortality of the troops which were sent from Europe to the colony was among other causes to be ascribed to the improper food, if considered with regard to the moist atmosphere, especially in Demerara; and that it became a paramount necessity to have the troops furnished with a greater portion of fresh meat than that allowed by the army regulations. These supplies of fresh meat are at present connected with heavy expenses to the treasury, the cattle being imported from the islands, chiefly from Puerto Rico, one of the Spanish colonies.

I alluded in former remarks to the fitness of the extensive savannahs between the rivers Berbice and Demerara, for grazing-grounds, and that they are much superior for that purpose to those of the Rupununi. The climate in these regions is uncommonly healthy, and the country so well watered by springs and rivulets, that the great want of water which exists in the savannahs of the Rupununi, and which is such an obstacle that I fear they will never be inhabited by Europeans or their offspring, is here entirely set aside. If, therefore, enterprising colonists should cultivate pasturing-grounds, and stock them with cattle from the savannahs of the Rio Branco, fresh beef might be had at an equally cheap rate as in the United States: it will then be in the power of the peasantry of British Guiana to provide themselves with fresh meat at a price which bears a relative value to their wages.

Fitness of savannahs between the rivers Berbice and Demerara for grazing-grounds.

The difficulties which might be connected with leading the cattle at the Rio Branco, to those savannahs between the rivers Demerara and Berbice, are comparatively few. They might be led across the savannahs to the foot of the mount Makarapan, where they might be embarked in bateaux or large canoes, which had been constructed for that purpose in the vicinity of Makarapan. The forests in these regions abound in crabwood; and if for the transporting of the cattle the period is chosen when the river is full, the cataracts are of little consequence: the large cataracts of the Orinoco are at that period passed in vessels of forty tons. The administrator of the Brazilian cattle-farms at the Rio Branco informed me, while staying at fort São Joaquim, that the number of cattle amounted to about five thousand, and that the price was six dollars per head. The pasture of the savannahs of the river Berbice being similar, and the localities and

Proposed plan of leading the cattle at the savannahs at the Rio Branco to the coast.

supply of water superior, to the savannahs of the Rio Branco, the success of farms which were stocked with that cattle would be ensured.

I cannot conclude my observations on the capabilities of British Guiana without referring once more to the importance of its timber trade, and the source of wealth which might be derived if there were a sufficient number of woodcutters. At present, if we make a few exceptions, it is only carried on by individuals who enter upon it with but little capital and slender means; and yet there are instances where the industrious and sober have reaped riches.

The fitness of the timbers for naval architecture is unparalleled, and in some instances is said to surpass the teak. The greenheart, the mora, and souari or sewarri, of all other woods are most unquestionably the best adapted for ship-building. Within the last ten or twelve years a considerable quantity of brown greenheart has been sent to Liverpool and Greenock; and I have been told that builders and others interested in shipping are now of opinion, after about ten years' trial of the wood, that in strength and durability it is superior to any oak, and it actually commands a higher price.

Had these woods been introduced and extensively employed in the royal dock-yards fifteen or twenty years ago, it is the opinion of competent judges that we should not now hear much of dry rot and Kyan's patent; and not to mention the rapid decay of vessels built of English and African oak, and the consequent frequent repairs, with what saving to Government would it not have been connected! If, therefore, the attention of the navy-board could be drawn to the important fact that British Guiana can furnish the finest and most durable wood in the world, in sufficient quantities to supply all the ship-building establishments in Great Britain, a double benefit would arise from it, namely, the saving to Government and the increased demand for the natural production of the colony. The first experiment might be made to establish a dock-yard for the repair of such of Her Majesty's cruisers on the West India station as draw not more than eighteen or nineteen feet water. The outlay of such an establishment would be trifling, if the importance of ultimate success be considered.

The woods which are qualified for ornamental purposes vie in elegance, if polished, with any in the world. The want of labourers is the great cause that these treasures lie comparatively hidden, and have scarcely excited attention. The demand in the colony has been so great for native woods, that those who are at present employed in that trade are not able to meet it.

III.

THE PRESENT CONDITION AND FUTURE PROSPECTS OF THE COLONY.

THE British colonies in the West Indies have been cultivated until recently by slave-labour; but England has since proclaimed the general emancipation of her former slaves throughout her colonial empire, and has set a bright example to Europe of erasing from the pages of her history one of the foulest blots.

The picture of the state of the colonies after a period of about two years since the eventful first of August 1838, cannot be contemplated with gratification by the planter, or by those who are interested in the agricultural prospects of the colony: there exists, no doubt, a rapid decrease, which does not refer to any individual colony, but is shared by all; and the most incontrovertible proofs lie in the contrast which the import of the single article of sugar into the United Kingdom, from the British West India and South American colonies, offers, if compared with former periods. The average annual import for the six years previous to 1836, amounted to 255,000 hogsheads; while in 1839 it has dwindled down to 179,800 hogsheads, showing a deficiency of 75,200 hogsheads, as compared with the average import of the former years, and of 42,300 hogsheads as compared with the import in 1838. It was not to be expected that the free labourer would devote himself with that ardour to the cultivation of products to which he was compelled while in slavery: still the deficiency is so great, that it must prove startling to even the warmest friends of that measure, which to execute, the nation gave twenty millions of pounds sterling.

The negroes evince the greatest indisposition to field labour: they have chosen to cultivate small patches of land, or if by industrious habits they have procured a small sum of money, they have become shopkeepers, petty traders, and hucksters. Now it must be generally acknowledged that the prosperity of the West India colonies was solely to be ascribed to the cultivation of those products for which the soil and climate adapted them: if these resources fall off, it must exercise the most distressing influence upon the population in general. No country can exist without a labouring class; and a nation of shopkeepers, petty traders, and hucksters, to the exclusion of the tiller of the soil, would be a phænomenon in political economy. If the prosperity of the colonies continue to decline with the rapidity of the last two years, that happiness, and advancement in religious instruction and civilization of the negroes, are not likely to follow, which the British nation at large expected when the great boon was tendered to the African. It cannot be denied that the colonists have done much in offering religion and education to the working classes; but will they continue to tax themselves, whilst they are deprived of the very means by which that taxation is supported? Or is the philanthropist sure that the seeds which religious teachers have sown in the breast of the African, have sufficiently prospered to expect fruit? or is it more likely that he will relapse to indifference towards religion, and adopt his former savage customs? His advancement in religion is the very basis on which the plans for his happiness have been founded; if that fail, the dangers of an unfettered condition of society will be united with indolence, the originator and companion of crime, and an unavoidable destruction of the colonies must succeed. Whether this would prove a matter of indifference to the people of Great Britain, is a question of sufficient importance to arrest our consideration.

The capital which is expended upon the culture of the British West India colonies belongs either directly to Great Britain or to the colonists, who are connected by origin, language, manners, and institutions, with England. The British possessions in the Western hemisphere are agricultural countries, in which manufactures do not thrive. Accustomed to the same habits and wants, and imbued with similar tastes as the English, they resorted to the mother country for the supply of manufactured goods, and such articles of luxury as they required and were within the reach of their circumstances; and while the trade of Great Britain with Europe had declined, from 1802 to 1836, from sixty-five to forty-eight per cent., the trade with the British colonies in America increased from eighteen to twenty-six per cent. The relative value of the export of goods of British manufacture to the colonial possessions is learned from Porter's parliamentary tables, according to which the exports to the British West Indies, with about nine hundred thousand inhabitants, surpassed in 1836 those to the British North American colonies, with a population of fifteen hundred thousand, by 1,050,000*l.* The respective amounts of exports to the British West Indies in 1836 were 3,786,453*l.*, to the British North American colonies, 2,732,291*l.* It appears by these tables, that Russia, with a population of sixty millions, receives British manufactures to the extent of only 5*d.*

per head; Prussia, with fourteen millions, $3\frac{1}{2}d.$ per head; Portugal, with three millions, and Spain, with fourteen millions, 8*d*. per head; Denmark, with two millions, and France, with thirty-two millions, 11*d*. per head; the United States of America, with fourteen millions, 17*s*. per head; the British North American colonies, with a population of a million and a half, 1*l*. 11*s*. 6*d*. per head; while the British West India colonies, with nine hundred thousand inhabitants, receive British manufactures to the extent of 3*l*. 12*s*. 6*d*. per head.

Continental Europe, actuated by the wish to protect her rival commercial establishments, throws every impediment in the way of introducing British manufactures; and in spite of all the reciprocity treaties which have been concluded with the continent, the exports to the states of Northern Europe, taken as a whole, is at present less that it was twenty-five years ago, while the reciprocity system has had the direct effect of destroying the British carrying-trade; and it is supposed that if this system is continued for ten or fifteen years longer, the British traffic with Europe will be carried on in foreign vessels. A similar danger threatens with regard to the United States, where in 1836 trade was carried on in two hundred and twenty-six British ships, or eighty-nine thousand three hundred tons, and in five hundred and twenty-four American ships, or two hundred and twenty-six thousand four hundred tons[*]. It is different with the British American and West Indian colonies, where not only the exports but likewise the tonnage returns have been rapidly increasing. The commercial crisis in 1811, when the export trade of England was only re-

[*] The number of vessels which arrived that year in British Guiana from Great Britain and the British colonies amounted to 614, or 101,440 tons.

stricted to its own colonies, had the most disastrous influence upon the nation at large, and the fall in the exports and imports, taken together for the one year, amounted to no less than thirty-six millions. " Now in order to appreciate the misery that would ensue to this country from a similar stoppage in its export trade at the present time, we have only to recollect, that our exports, which in 1810 were forty-three millions, had in 1838 risen to one hundred and five millions; and that our imports, which in 1809 were thirty-one millions, had risen in 1838 to sixty-one millions; and that our population, which at the former period was seventeen millions, is now twenty-five. If such wide-spread and heart-rending misery was produced then, what would be its effects now, when the manufacturing establishments of the country have nearly tripled, and our manufacturing population has advanced in a proportion unheard of in any other country*?"

If we look at the political relations of Great Britain, it is only to be wondered at that hostilities have not broken out as yet with the continental powers or the United States, who are watching her with the greatest jealousy, ready to avail themselves of the first opportunity to commence the contest. Whenever this crisis may arrive, with all the predicted evils in its train, the colonies will remain under these circumstances the only resource upon which Great Britain can reckon for a market for its manufactures, and for an employment of her merchant navy.

This is the importance which is attached to the colonies, and therefore it should be the particular care of Great Britain to foster their interests, and to remedy the declining state of her emancipated colonies.

Sugar and coffee have become necessaries of life; and it follows, that if our own colonies, under the present

* Blackwood's Magazine for December, 1839.

system of free labour, are not able to produce an adequate supply, recourse must be had to the tropical states of South America, where sugar, coffee, and molasses are cultivated by slaves. The prosperity, in a commercial respect, of the foreign slave colonies is materially increased, and American, nay even British capital, for the cultivation of sugar and coffee, has been invested to a great extent.

France and Holland have awaited the result of emancipation; and should any failure be connected with the free-labour system in the British colonies, they will pause before they tender emancipation to their slaves. Spain and the Brazils were never sincere in their promise to abolish the slave trade, or even to ameliorate the wretched condition of their slaves. Even if it were desirable, for the purpose of carrying into effect the philanthropic views of the nation, and for the sake of the emancipated labourer, and in order to indulge him in his habitual indolence, to sacrifice the British West India colonies, and to sink the capital which has been vested in their culture, their downfall would be the deathblow to the hope of suppressing the most frightful scourge, the basest of all trades, the trade in human beings, which under existing circumstances, has already received a new impetus. It is positively asserted, that notwithstanding all the exertions of Great Britain, and the vigilance of her navy, there are so many chances of a slaver escaping, that thousands of slaves continue to be imported in Cuba and Puerto Rico. The most effectual means of checking the slave trade is to render it unprofitable, and this may be effected by producing sugar by the labour of free men at a cheaper rate than it can be produced by the labour of slaves. The remedy is easy and obvious; it consists in a well-organized system of emigration from those places where there is a surplus population, and the inhabitants of which are found to be best suited for a tropical climate.

From these general views, which affect the whole British colonies in South America, we revert to that magnificent province, to the description of which our foregoing pages were dedicated.

The last trace of slavery terminated in Guiana on the first of August 1838, by a bill having passed the court of policy, or legislative body, which had for its object the abolition of the negro apprenticeship on that day, unfettered by any restriction, and unconnected with any subsidiary enactments.

It was to be expected, that men who had been held, all their lives, to compulsory labour, should be disposed to relax, and in some instances totally abstain from it; but it was scarcely thought, that in a colony like Guiana, where labour was comparatively easy as contrasted with that on a sugar estate at the mountainous islands; and where, besides, every contrivance which machinery could devise to ease manual labour had been introduced,—that the failure of crops would have been so frightful. The first decrease arose from unfavourable weather, and from the circumstance, that the negro, unaccustomed to the new state of things, did not understand his new position: but it soon became evident that an irregularity of labour existed, and that the planter could not be certain of the same number of labourers in the field two days together; and many of the negroes, after working for a short time, left their work in order to follow their own inclinations. Another diminution arose from the indisposition of the women to attend to field work; and though on many of the estates, throughout British Guiana, a fair portion of labour was obtained, the decrease in 1838, as compared with the average crop of the six previous years, was 9664 hogsheads of sugar. The deficiency in the exports of the first quarter of the year 1839, as compared with that of 1838, amounted to 1238 hogsheads, and was ascribed to the excessive drought, which lasted for upwards of seventy days without respite, in consequence of which the savannahs, creeks, or lakes, were dried up, and the trenches, having no supply, were exhausted; while the sugar-canes were left uncut from the impossibility of conveying them to the works. The decrease in export for Demerara and Essequibo continued, and amounted, during the second quarter of 1839, as compared with the average quantity of the corresponding quarters of 1831, 1832, and 1833, to 4473 hogsheads of sugar, 2565 puncheons of rum, 4086 hogsheads of molasses, and 576,060lbs. of coffee: however, "the lengthened drought of the last and beginning of the present quarter would have caused diminished crops in Essequibo and Demerara under the most coerced system of labour. The coffee-berry is fixed, and a large harvest is anticipated." Thus reports Governor Light to the Marquis of Normanby, on 16th of July 1839. The exports during the third quarter, namely, from the 6th of July to the 10th of October, as compared with the average quantity of the corresponding quarters of 1831, 1832, and 1833, prove unfortunately a decrease of 7720 hogsheads (12,660,800lbs.) of sugar, 2116 puncheons of rum, 7309 hogsheads of molasses, and 1,271,878lbs. of coffee. The deficiency in the coffee crop after the large harvest which three months previously was anticipated, is startling, and is decisive of the proof, that not only the unfavourable season, but the general idleness and want of labour had a great share in the unfortunate results of the first year of freedom.

On the causes which produced that deficiency, I cannot do better than quote the opinion of one of the ablest statesmen of the present time :—

"I am not disposed as a general proposition to refer this falling off in the produce to the want of adequate wages as its cause. Many vexatious disputes have no doubt arisen: the proper rate of wages was all to seek: the engagements and obligations of slavery had left strong traces in the habits and minds both of employer and negro; the one, with little reason, expected that the negro was, at all events, to carry on the cultivation of sugar; while the other, with as little right, thought he was, in any case, to remain in undisturbed possession of his large provision-ground. But a larger or more general cause had led to the decline of cultivation of sugar and coffee. * * * *

"A few acres of ground will produce provisions for a family with some surplus to sell at market, and bring home manufactured goods; the negroes who earn high wages, buy or hire plots of land, and refuse to let their daily labour for hire."

To this circumstance, coupled with the indolence to which a great part of the negroes are prone, must be ascribed the want of continuous and regular labour; and consequently the deficiency in exports amounted, at the close of the year 1839, to 467,480*l.*, as compared with 1838, which year in itself left a deficiency in Demerara alone, exclusive of Berbice, to no less an amount than 930,000*l.* as compared with 1837. The conclusion is fallacious, that supposing the exports of sugar for the year 1839 reach only 35,000 hogsheads, the returns in money will be larger than when the produce was at its greatest extent. The very important fact, that the expenses of producing a hogshead of sugar are increased in equal ratio to its higher value in the market, does not leave sufficient profit to the planter to counterbalance the diminished quantity of his produce. Experienced planters fear that the falling off in the crops in the present year will be much greater, since the labour which the planter was able to procure was only applied to the cutting of the ripe canes, while planting, drainage, and other labour for securing future crops were neglected; and it is therefore to be foreseen that the cultivation of the soil, which has been already neglected, will in a short time be entirely abandoned, if some remedy be not devised to replace those labourers who have become independent, or follow other pursuits than field labour in order to procure their livelihood.

An unlimited and free emigration alone is able to rescue British Guiana from its rapid decline. Emigration alone will enable us to reap all the advantages which this truly magnificent colony offers; a colony, which as at present situated, exports with a population of 100,000 labourers 35,000 hogsheads of sugar; while Jamaica, with 440,000 labourers, produces only 53,100 hogsheads; and Barbadoes, with 90,000 coloured labourers, 23,500 hogsheads; a fact which forcibly points out the superior fertility of British Guiana. This colony surpasses equally in imports every other in the British West Indies, and the import of goods of British manufacture amounted in 1836 to £5 14s. per head, and have probably risen in 1839 to £10 per head.

If the misery which would be inflicted upon the large manufacturing towns might be calculated from the effects which the stoppage of the export trade caused in 1810 and 1811, the prospects of the manufacturing districts in England, in the case of the breaking out of any war with Europe or with the United States, are distressing.

It becomes therefore the double policy of Great Britain to foster the resources of her own possessions, in order to increase with her population the demand for her manufactured goods; and the example of British Guiana, where in 1838, under the most adverse circumstances, the increasing demands for manufactured goods and other supplies had occasioned an additional tonnage inwards of 10,618 tons as compared with that of 1836, will point again to that colony as the mart where the manufactured goods of the mother country are likely to find the readiest sale. There is every fear that the growing manufacturing establishments on the continent of Europe may shut out British goods from the European market; and how far the European powers are anxious to accomplish this, the Prussico-Teutonic commercial league and Russian ukases have sufficiently shown. In the colonies alone, from long-continued habits and connexions of their population, the supply of British manufactures meets no competition from foreigners.

In the British West Indies, Barbadoes is the only colony which is thickly peopled. Its population is computed at 104,000 inhabitants upon an area of one hundred and fifty square miles, or six hundred and ninety-three inhabitants to each square mile. The population is therefore in such a proportion, that the relation between the employer and the labourer is put upon a natural level; and it is generally considered that in consequence the free labour system will best succeed in that colony. In order to accomplish the desirable object of raising British Guiana to the state of the island of Barbadoes with regard to its population, it remains to point out those sources from which labourers may be obtained, who are suited for working under a tropical clime.

Africa is the part of the world which for upwards of

three centuries supplied the colonies of European nations with labourers. Abounding in a population which, buried in the darkness of savage life, were divided in numerous tribes engaged in constant warfare with each other, we will leave the question entirely untouched, whether religion and civilization have gained by the drafts which European nations have made upon those unfortunate beings. The ties of relationship and country were not torn asunder for making them converts to religion and civilization; cupidity was the mainspring of those acts for which history will ever blush.

Plans have been proposed to establish steam navigation, and to invite the most intelligent natives of the African coast to visit Guiana, in order that they may judge for themselves whether it offer any advantages which cannot be procured in Africa; and communicate their experience to their own countrymen; by which means not only a stream of free emigrants might be obtained, but the success of this scheme would be equally calculated to further the views of civilizing Africa.

The short passage in steamers between the coast of Africa and Guiana, might induce many to give their assistance in getting in the crops, and return after having earned a sum of wages, which according to their idea renders them rich. The orderly and religious state of the indigenous labouring population in Guiana could not fail to have the best effects upon the minds of the newly arrived Africans; and at their return to their homes, with the good example of their black brethren in Guiana before their eyes, a powerful means would be given of disseminating religious principles and civilization among them. In this way the philanthropic views of Mr. Buxton and his coadjutors would be promoted. The planter in Guiana, however, could not calculate upon the timely arrival of this assistance, which would be always subjected to circumstances and caprices; and although many might settle permanently, and amalgamate with the existing creole race, this process is too slow to warrant the expectation of much benefit for the colony. The most important question to decide in adopting such a plan as an auxiliary scheme of providing Guiana with the necessary labour is, whether it would meet the approbation of the British Government?

If the question be calmly considered, the plan appears plausible, and deserves to receive the approbation of the British Government, much as it might be opposed, for well-founded reasons, to the entire transfer of Africans to an American colony. Under their protection, measures might be adopted to facilitate this periodical emigration; and its very nature, that not a permanent settlement, but merely their labour for a certain period is aimed at, excludes even the shadow of compulsion. Ireland, and several districts on the continent of Europe, offer similar examples; and the assertion of the same right which the Irish labourer has at his option, if he considers himself wronged by his employer in England, might be applied n a still higher degree to the African, who offers his temporary labour to the colonist.

The peculiar situation of Great Britain in whatever relates to the suppression of the slave trade, makes it, I fear, impracticable to recruit at the coast of Africa for permanent settlers. Whatever might be the advantages which might accrue to the African races from a permanent settlement at Guiana, the evil genius of the slave trade has spread its wings over benighted Africa, and the best intentions for the amelioration of its barbarous population run the risk of being accused of selfish views. The plans of the African colonization society share a similar suspicion, and are said to be undertaken merely as the first germs of African colonies under British sway. The treasures of the soil, of which that vast region might be made the depository, and the reward of industry and social amelioration which await the African from the realization of Mr. Buxton's plans, are as much exposed to the mistrust of other European nations, as the scheme of transferring the African for the same purpose to Guiana, where there is a field sufficiently extensive for millions to reap the fruits of their industry and the blessings of the Christian religion and civilization, and where the savage would advance in the career of civilization with greater rapidity than could ever be expected in Africa.

More effective measures however are requisite, than those offered by the prospect of distant success in recruiting labourers from Africa, in order to arrest the present decline of our colonies in the West, and to stay the increase of the slave trade, which in consequence of that decline has received a new impetus. I need only to point to Cuba and Puerto Rico for the proof of the latter assertion, where American and British capital reap all the advantages of a continued slave trade and an ample supply of labourers. The prosperity of these colonies is unfortunately built upon the downfall of the British colonies, suffering as they do the most urgent want of labourers for their rich and luxuriant lands; and the only hope which is left for averting this rapid decline of the colonies, is the proposition of introducing a number of Indian labourers, called Hill Coolies. It appears that this poor race has been subjected to the most abject state of degradation; and if we can believe the public accounts, want prevailed in the British Indian possessions in 1838 to such a degree, that five hundred thousand of these miserable beings are said to have died of hunger. They migrate in India annually in large numbers in search of employment, which appears to be precarious, while, if successful, their earnings yield a bare subsistence. It was therefore imagined by some parties interested in British Guiana, that if these Hill Coolies, who were starving, were to emigrate to Guiana, where an unlimited demand for labour would ensure them high wages, they would not only profit themselves, but also the colony which was to receive their labour. Four hundred and thirty-seven Coolies embarked, therefore, in Calcutta, of whom sixteen died on the voyage, and two fell overboard in a violent gale; while four hundred and nineteen landed in Guiana. Their terms of contract were five years, service for wages of five rupees monthly, payable in dollars at the exchange of two rupees per dollar; they were to be supplied daily with provisions, and annually with clothing; as also with medical attendance and medicines.

It is much to be regretted that no proper selection was made among those who offered their services, and that necessary precautions were not taken at their arrival to prevent the diseases, which more abundant food, change of climate, herding together in one room in lieu of separate houses, and working at the fields without being inured to the climate, were likely to cause. If some regulation had been in operation for that purpose, it is not likely that the sickness which spread so widely and proved so fatal to the Coolies would have occurred[*]. It was in consequence, that the commissaries appointed by the Governor

[*] According to the official returns of the stipendiary magistrate, dated November 1st, 1839, the number of deaths which had occurred among the Coolies since they landed amounted to sixty-three males and three females.

of British Guiana to inquire into the state and condition and general treatment of emigrants, recommended that all emigrants, on their arrival in the colony, should not be permitted to be located on any estate, or elsewhere, until the agent for emigrants, or some other person appointed for that purpose, first see and ascertain that the dwellings to be appropriated for their reception are in every way suitable and comfortable; that the labour required of them should be apportioned to their several circumstances; that they should not be called upon to perform a full day's work for several months after their arrival; and if practicable, the wages allowed to them should not be less, in proportion to the labour performed, than is paid to the other labouring classes of the community. This recommendation was adopted by the Governor, who observes on this subject, in his despatch to the Marquis of Normanby, dated Demerara, 14th October, 1839,—" The anxiety to meet the views of Her Majesty's Government, expressed by the community at large on the subject of immigration, will enable Your Lordship to assume any position in protection of immigrants you may think necessary. I have already given directions respecting the reception of immigrants introduced by private speculators, who have hitherto detained them on board till located. The harbour-master is instructed to secure immediate communication with the shore, and disembarkation within twenty-four hours of arrival in the river*."

It cannot be denied that the loss of life by mismanagement at the first arrival of the Coolies proved serious to them as a body. Much of it was to be ascribed to the

* Parliamentary paper, "Hill Coolies, British Guiana," ordered to be printed 21st of February, 1840, p. 45.

difficulty of inducing them to submit to timely remedies, and to the experience of medical men; but this aversion has been overcome, and wise regulations with regard to their welfare have produced happy results. Indeed it is evident, that with the exception of the African, they appear to be better qualified as labourers in Guiana than any other individuals. It is represented by official reports that every attention is paid to render them comfortable, and from all the information which was procured by the commissioners appointed for the purpose of inquiring into their present state, it appeared that they had considerably improved since their arrival. They execute their work with a cheerfulness not to be exceeded in any part of the world; many of them say, "We feel so content and comfortable here, that if our families were with us, we should prefer remaining in this country. We get more food and are better taken care of than in our own country." Anunto Ram, the head Sirdar, an intelligent man, and who has recently married a young woman from a Coolie family on this estate (Highbury in Berbice), remarks, "I have only my father and my mother in India, and I will go to Calcutta at any time my master wishes, and return with plenty of these people: they would be glad to come here*."

In comparing the mortality since their arrival with the Europeans, it is as one to three; their blood is purer than that of the negroes, and the observations of the colonial surgeon on the cases from Bellevue is, that the same sort of sores in a negro would not have been cured so easily†. Indeed Dr. Smith, of whom Governor Light observes, that "his character and principles place him

---

* Parliamentary paper, "Hill Coolies, British Guiana," p. 8.
† Ibid. p. 4.

above all suspicion of expressing an opinion respecting the Coolies from interested motives," reports to him, "I beg leave to say that I entertain a more favourable opinion of the constitution of the Coolies, in reference to their adaptation to this climate, than any other class of immigrants whom I have met in the colony. Of the thirty Coolies, including the interpreter and two cooks, placed under my charge, none have been attacked since the 7th of June with the intermittent fever, the endemic of British Guiana; nor do any seem to have suffered prior to that period from this cause. This community, when compared with the Maltese and Portuguese immigrants, is worthy of note." * * * *

"The uncommon rapidity with which most of those severe cases (of ulceration) progressed to a favourable termination, is a negative proof of the non-predisposition of the Coolies to the disease generally termed in this colony 'constitutional ulcer,' while it affords strong evidence of the great restorative powers of their constitutions, surpassing that of every other class of labourers whom I have had occasion to treat for the same disease in this country*."

Governor Light, in a despatch to Lord John Russell, dated 6th of December 1839, says—

"It is certain that Christianity is beginning to have its effect on the Coolies: those who were in the colonial hospital at first required their food at the hands of persons of their own caste; in a few days they lost that feeling; when prayers were read in the hospital by the attendant clergyman, they were attentive and respectful hearers. More than one, on his death bed, received the consolation of the Christian minister, at their request; and one particularly, in his dying moments, told the clergyman he

* Parliamentary paper, "Hill Coolies, British Guiana," pp. 13, 14.

was happy, and prepared to go to God, from what he had heard him say*." The concluding paper of these interesting despatches, which refer to the state and condition of the Hill Coolies in British Guiana, affords high satisfaction; namely, a general return compiled from the stipendiary magistrate's monthly reports, respecting the Hill Coolies, dated the 1st of December, 1839, from which we learn that no death had occurred, and that the returns are highly favourable for the past month, not exhibiting a single case of serious illness; and among those reported sick, but few had been more than one day in the hospital: no instance had occurred of any Coolie having left his estate to prefer a complaint; nor had the district magistrates, on their periodical inspection, any grievance brought to their notice†.

This is a document, which, in connection with the foregoing extracts, will prove the incalculable benefit which would accrue to thousands, nay millions, if it should seem good to Her Majesty's Government to permit a further introduction of Coolies into British Guiana. Christianity would receive its numerous converts, and a body of useful labourers would be introduced, who by constitution appear to be admirably adapted for the colony.

It is not probable that any number of emigrants which are likely to arrive in British Guiana would reduce wages. For want of labour, thousands of acres of the most fertile land have been abandoned. The whole seacoast of the Berbice river, and between this and the Corentyn, was once in cultivation; and the number of abandoned estates in the Corentyn alone amounts to fifty-eight out of eighty.

* Parliamentary paper, "Hill Coolies, British Guiana," p. 51.
† Ibid. p. 55.

The British side of the Corentyn has only three estates, and from information which Governor Light received on the spot, the same advantages of rich alluvial soil fit for sugar cultivation are offered for sixty miles above the extreme estate, Skeldon*, and might average one hundred thousand hogsheads of sugar. The cultivable soil on the east bank of the Berbice river is equally rich for a hundred miles above Mara, thirty miles from New Amsterdam†. The Dutch formerly cultivated the banks of the Essequibo a hundred miles above its embouchure; if we except the three islands at the mouth of the river, cultivation does not extend at present five miles beyond its mouth. The same remarks apply to the rich coast land of the rivers Pomeroon and Marocco. But without extending the cultivation, it requires thousands of labourers to restore the sugar cultivation, which has suffered within the last two years. Indeed British Guiana wants a population of fifty-five millions of inhabitants, to people it as thickly as Barbadoes; there is therefore sufficient scope for an unlimited number of emigrants, without supplanting or competing with those who still remain engaged in tilling the soil.

The Coolies who are starving in their own country, and who are qualified by constitution and habits for the task, are still the most eligible labourers for Guiana; and although Government appears to be averse, for reasons which have been assigned, to transfer them from India to British Guiana, still those reasons are not so well founded as to enforce acquiescence. It depends upon the Government to devise the more efficacious and more simple measures which would remove the present

* Skeldon produced during the period of apprenticeship of the labourers from eight to nine hundred hogsheads of sugar.

† Parliamentary papers relative to the West Indies, Part I. 1839, p. 279.

objections. A new system of slavery can never rise again in a British colony; and the best argument in favour of enabling the crowded population of India to take advantage of the high wages of Guiana, lies in the unrivalled fertility of the soil, the British capital ready to be embarked to call forth the fruits of that fertility, and the wish of the inhabitants and those interested in the colony to adopt whatever the British Government has to propose for the advancement of emigration.

"The experience of the past, the fears for the future, will enable your Lordship to fix any condition for protection of emigrants in this colony. 'Give us the means of keeping up our present cultivation, and we will accede to every wish of Her Majesty's Government,' is the general sentiment of the respectable portion of the community.*"

There are many authenticated instances on record which directly contradict the statements which have been made in England;—that the labourers in British Guiana were not liberally treated by their employers, who seemed disposed to oppress them, and thus prevent their taking the full advantage of their freedom. I choose, however, only the two following, as a proof that emancipation is producing its effects without opposition. Sixty-three labourers, the greater number of whom are headmen and mechanics, purchased, in November 1839, the estate Northbrook, on the east coast of Demerara, consisting of five hundred acres of land, for which they paid ten thousand dollars (equal to two thousand pounds sterling), and they were enabled to pay the purchase-money principally from their savings, since they obtained freedom on the first of August 1838. The labourers of Mr. Blair in the county of Berbice, bought the estate No. 6, or

* Governor Light's Despatch to the Marquis of Normanby, dated 14th of October, 1839.

Bel-Air, with plantain cultivation and a large dwelling-house, for fifty thousand guilders (equal to three thousand five hundred pounds sterling).

Would our labouring classes in Europe be ever able to amass riches sufficient to become landed proprietors? Doomed to pine and toil in poverty, in rags, and hardships, their only landed possession is likely to be the grave which closes their misery. Would that they availed themselves of the advantages which a colony like British Guiana offers to them!

I cannot but insert here, in its place, the opinion of a man, who, for his piety and learning, is an ornament to the Church over which he presides as prelate :—

" I have been much struck, as I passed from parish to parish (in British Guiana), with the appearance of the people, with the respectability of their dress, and with the quietness and propriety of their demeanour. Their behaviour at the consecration of the several churches, and chapel-schools, and burial-grounds, and whilst partaking in or witnessing the rite of confirmation, was serious and becoming; whilst the promptness and largeness of their pecuniary subscriptions to the several places of public worship and religious instruction manifest the piety of their feelings, and the personal comfort of their present condition. At one temporary chapel of ease, the sum of fifty pounds was collected for the purchase of an organ, in the course of two hours from the time it was mentioned to them. At the church of St. Swithin's no less a sum than thirty joes (equal to forty-seven pounds sterling) was raised for the inclosure, with iron rails, of the tomb of their deceased minister; a proof not less of pecuniary competence than of a tender and grateful recollection: and at the Kitty chapel-school the liquidation of a debt of one hundred and fifty pounds sterling has been undertaken by the people of the surrounding estates, to secure its immediate consecration. At St. Saviour's, on the Aberdeen estate, Essequibo, the labourers alone on six of the neighbouring estates contributed towards the erection of the chapel-school upwards of three thousand three hundred and ninety-four guilders, equal to two hundred and forty-two pounds sterling.

"When the labouring classes of any community can lay by so largely, and spend their earnings so holily and usefully, there must be a spirit working within them, which under judicious and affectionate guidance will settle down into a habit of contented and steady industry.*"

Can civilized England offer so bright an example among its labouring population as is here recorded of the people of British Guiana?

And why are not such advantages to be offered to the crowded population of India, the poor starving Coolie, who, reclaimed from human misery, may become as useful a citizen as many of the present labourers, the former neglected slaves of British Guiana? They are seeking employment to save themselves from starvation. A climate similar to that of Calcutta, and wages three times as high as they can ever obtain at home, instruction in the Christian religion, and competency, are offered to them as inducements to dispose of their labour to a British colony; and in order to satisfy the most scrupulous, all arrangements about their conveyance, the contracts for their employment, their housing, food, clothing, and whatever may be connected with their welfare, is left to the arrangements of the Government, and is to be conducted by their agents at the expense of the colony. The

* A Charge delivered to the clergy of the English Church in British Guiana, by the Right Reverend William Hart, Bishop of Barbadoes and the Leeward Islands. Demerara, 1839, p. 7 to 8.

conveyance from Calcutta to Guiana is less, by about one-fourth, than the voyage from Liverpool to Australia; and should the projected communication between the Atlantic and Pacific Ocean, by means of the Isthmus of Darien, be realized, and steam navigation come into operation, Georgetown in Demerara may be reached in twenty days from Calcutta.

The negroes captured in slave ships have been hitherto carried for adjudication of the mixed commission, to the colonies of foreign powers, as to Surinam, Cuba, and the Brazils. The miseries experienced by those in Cuba are appalling. According to the late expositions of Mr. Turnbull, the poor captured Africans, if emancipated at Havannah, were handed over to the Spanish authorities, who hired them out for seven years to the best bidder. The necessary consequence was, that the party who engaged their services had not even an interest in keeping them alive after the lapse of that period, and they lay under no obligation, either legal or conventional, to support them when disabled by sickness or accident. Nay, it is asserted, that when death occurred among the slaves at the plantations where the emancipated African was hired, his name was substituted in the bill of mortality, and he remained a slave for life under the denomination of him who died in reality. According to the old system, these unfortunate captives, if even nominally free, were instantly hurried into an abyss of misery more deplorable and more desperate than that of the regularly imported African*.

Indeed, the apprehensions of the British Government, that their policy in putting down the slave-trade would be

* Travels in the West, Cuba; with Notices of Porto Rico, and the Slave Trade. By David Turnbull, Esq., M.A., London, 1840.

exposed to suspicion, by making large addition to their rich colonies of the negroes captured in slave-ships, and that they might be told that Great Britain was indirectly recruiting her own possessions with compulsory labour by the very means which they employed to suppress the traffic of other nations,—ought to be waived, after the exposition of the atrocious system which is pursued in Cuba by the Spanish authorities. Of all the governments who have promised their co-operation to put down the horrible traffic in human beings, Great Britain alone has acted honestly and strenuously to effect it. There can be no doubt that these unfortunate rescued beings would be better treated in every respect if they were brought to British Guiana, which province has the additional recommendation of being within reach of a voyage of only a few days, and the cost of the bounty paid for captures would be readily reimbursed by the colony; while they would thus be placed under British law and protection, and not be subjected to a hopeless condition, and to the abuses of the word emancipation in a Spanish colony or in the Brazilian territory.

The expenses for transport and maintenance of captured slaves, who are sent annually from the Bahamas to Honduras, might be materially lessened to Government if they were transmitted at the expense of the colony to British Guiana. The population at the Bahamas must be ample enough, otherwise these Africans would not be sent to Honduras.

A new hope has arisen to the colonists of Guiana of increasing the population of that province by coloured emigrants from the United States, where in spite of the clamour of liberty and equality, people of colour are oppressed and despised. A local or voluntary subscription immigration society has been formed for that purpose;

and the arrival of two delegates, chosen and appointed by a general meeting of the free coloured population of the city of Baltimore and state of Maryland, in order to ascertain the character of the climate of British Guiana, its natural productions, and the political and social conditions of the coloured inhabitants of the province, will, it is hoped, have the best effects in inducing the wronged race in the United States to migrate to British Guiana, where there is no distinction of colour, where they may participate in the same esteem and the same public rights which are in the reach of the European or any other emigrant.

The colony offers them other advantages. The climate is well adapted to their constitutions; and with industrious habits, an independence may be acquired in a shorter time than in any other part of the world; and here the blessings of education, and full liberty to worship the Creator according to the dictates of conscience, may be procured unfettered, and without reference to race or complexion.

One of the great advantages which is likely to arise to the colony from the migration of American labourers to British Guiana, is that it will exercise a favourable effect on the other labourers in the colony. The task which the American emigrants perform in Trinidad amounted in one instance to three times the quantity of labour formally extracted from the unwilling slave; and it is stated that this produced a favourable effect on the other labourers on the estate where the American emigrants were employed.

The planter has been hitherto at the mercy of the labourer, who, well aware that his occupation was in full demand, uséd no exertions to obtain the approbation of his employer. If he was discharged, he was sure of being received with open arms at the neighbouring estate. This will in some respect be remedied by the arrival of American emigrants, or by a greater supply of free labour; and if the present labourer do not wish to verge on a state of barbarism, and to relinquish his comfortable house and bed, his showy dress and little luxuries, he is in self-defence obliged to adopt more industrious habits. I think that competition, more than any other means, will induce the indigenous labouring classes to settle down into steady habits of industry.

The indolence of the aboriginal inhabitants of Guiana, the Indians, and their present wandering habits, have presented great obstacles to the colony. This aversion of accepting employment from the colonists may have arisen, in a great measure, from the impositions to which they were formerly exposed, and where for the sake of a few glass beads, knives, &c., to the amount of a few shillings, they were kept at hard work for months. These impositions have now almost subsided, and the Indian population near the coast regions have become of great assistance to woodcutters, where they are employed in cutting and squaring timber, splitting shingles, &c. It is evident that they can labour, and the opinion which the most experienced woodcutters possess of the comparative value of Indians and negroes, as labourers, is in favour of the former. Practices have been in existence to secure an Indian as a labourer, which are by no means creditable. It would be advisable for his advancement in civilization to awaken in him a demand for decent apparel and other comforts of civilized nations; and by exalting him in his own opinion, and increasing his self-respect, his industry would be called forth to keep up the standing he had acquired.

The Indian, uncontaminated by European vices, and that bane, rum, is strictly moral. The European colonists owe to these poor neglected races a large and long debt. They possessed themselves of their land; employed them, at their first arrival, on the cultivation of those fertile tracts; and when the African slave was substituted for the Indian labourer, and the necessity for the further services of the aborigines ceased, they were driven to the wilds of the interior and neglected. It is therefore a slight retribution for wrongs committed in former days by Europeans, to spread religious principles among the remnant of those once powerful tribes, and to convert them to that state of civilization which is in their reach.

Such philanthropic measures ought to be disinterested and merely to be considered in the light of repaying an old debt. But setting this aside, it offers advantages to the colony. The numerous tribes, the Macusis, Wapisianas, and Arecunas, who inhabit the tributaries of the upper Essequibo, are powerful; and if these poor beings are once converted—and we know that with religion, civilization and industrious habits go hand in hand—if not the present, the future generation may be induced, when thus qualified to come and settle among the colonists, to assist by the labour of their hands to the prosperity of the colony.

There are some serious impediments which have operated against the establishment of religious teachers amongst the races at our undetermined boundary; these obstacles it is hoped will be removed by wise provisions of Her Majesty's Government, whom the enslaved African already thanks for liberty, and upon whom the Indian, with equal confidence, trusts for his amelioration.

Great Britain is considered to be oppressed with a superabundant population; and the evils resulting from a mass of human beings restricted for their subsistence to so narrow a space, might be counteracted, it has been thought, by emigration on a large scale. Ministers have already taken measures to effect this, and the new Colonization Commission is directed to afford every assistance for that purpose. The stream of emigration has been hitherto directed to New South Wales and the adjacent colonies, and has been accompanied by such a rapid development, that the number of emigrants, who amounted nine years ago to fifteen hundred, has increased in 1838 to fifteen thousand. Although Australia may offer advantages to the emigrant, the distance from the mother country; the circumstance that he who embarks for that distant colony tears himself for ever from his country and relations; the hostile tribes who oppose the settlers, cold winters, and, not least, the want of water in many districts—are points of weighty consideration. Even famine has not been unknown in some settlements; and the distress of the poor in October last year, and the extent of sufferings in consequence of scarcity, appear to have been appalling. In Hobart Town hundreds of children of both sexes, more than half-naked, starving at the most inclement season of the year from want of food, of fuel, of everything, were driven at daylight every morning forth from the nightly abode of undescribable wretchedness, to allay the cravings of hunger as means might be obtained. "Charity is the only resource; employment there is none to be obtained; and if there was, what labour could such children perform, so as to obtain for them even an adequate support[*]?"

Such misery is foreign to British Guiana. Throughout this rich and beautiful country there is an equable cli-

[*] Colonial Times (published in Hobart Town), October 8, 1839. See Colonial Gazette, February 5, 1840.

mate, and nature's bounty is so great that poor rates are unknown.

It is recommended to the Commissioners of Colonization, " that other circumstances being equal, the most desirable emigrants for New South Wales would be young married couples without children, and that the commissioners should aim at sending out young people with few children: but although the latter might eventually become a valuable acquisition to the colony, nevertheless the wants of the colonists for available labour were urgent, and required an immediate rather than a prospective supply."

Let us see what advantages British Guiana offers to a father of a large family, who has resolved upon emigration to distant parts. " Coffee plantations," it is observed in a colonial paper from Guiana, " are peculiarly fitted for giving employment to all ages of both sexes. The poor of Ireland, England, and Scotland, who have large families, in thousands of instances cannot avail themselves of the assistance of their children in the prosecution of their labour, because in country districts, particularly where agriculture is the chief employment, strong hands are required; so that the young and the weak are deprived of the opportunity to contribute anything towards their own support; but should a thousand poor labouring men, each with a family of ten, arrive in this colony, they could get work for every one of them that was able to pluck a coffee-berry. A coffee-picker, working at a reasonable rate, may earn a dollar a day; the business is so easy and light, that it could be performed by little boys and girls."

It is well known that a voyage to Australia occupies four to five months; Guiana may be reached in a sailing-vessel in five weeks, and a company called the West Indian Steam Navigation Company has lately been organized for opening a rapid, commodious, and regular communication with the rich and fertile colonies of the British empire in the west, by steamers, by means of which Demerara may be reached in the course of from sixteen to eighteen days. Generations may elapse before it will be possible to establish so rapid a communication with the colonies in Australia.

The equipment necessary for emigrating to British Guiana is trifling if compared with what is required for proceeding to New South Wales or the Canadas. The length and the severity of the winters, and the necessity of providing for the first year provision and clothing, as the resources of the soil can only be rendered available after a long period, are of weighty consideration.

The extensive landholder and manufacturer of sugar and the labourer constitute the two great classes of the population in British Guiana; the middle classes, so necessary to connect the two extremes, are almost entirely wanting. The emigrant who could command a moderate capital is best adapted for filling that void. His attention would be directed to the cultivation of such commodities as do not require vast outlays or much manual labour. In the preceding part I have already alluded to the cultivation of tea, spices of all kinds, tobacco, indigo, arnatto, the grape-vine, cocoa, rice, plantains, and maize, as demanding less capital and less manual labour than the sugar-cane. The extensive cultivation of tropical fruits, and chiefly the pine-apple, which with the approaching establishment of steam-boats might be imported extensively into Great Britain, would afford competence to many.

I revert again to the great importance of an extensive cultivation of cotton in Guiana, where there are lands near the coast and in the interior for raising the finest kinds. If for political reasons it were desirable to counterbalance the great injury which must accrue to Great Britain from a decreased importation of that necessary article for manufactures, caused either by internal convulsions of the slave states, or by war with this country, Guiana offers an unlimited field for its cultivation. If such a period should ever arrive, the increased population which would be required to cultivate it to the demanded extent would cause a larger import of British manufactures, and indemnify Great Britain for the loss which she would sustain in the United States, where the capitalists of New England aspire already, by the establishment of extensive manufactories, to effect the exclusion of British goods.

It is much to be wondered at that the extraordinary facilities which the colony of British Guiana offers for colonization have not promoted an extensive emigration of industrious Europeans to this territory. The fecundity of its soil, and the great energy of vegetation between the tropics, ensures the agriculturist a succession of harvests; no winter interferes to impede his labour, no blighting hurricane thwarts his prospects, no earthquake spreads horror and desolation over the scene of his industry. A uniform climate reigns throughout the year, and the soil possesses unequalled richness, and extends for several hundred miles from the coast, washed by the Atlantic, to the sources of those rivers, which, if population could be planted on their banks, would offer means for the maintenance of millions, and facilities for the most extensive inland navigation.

We know, from the history of former and modern times, that countries have sunk in commercial respect, whose internal communication was rendered difficult, although their fertility was great. The facility which the rivers of Guiana afford for inland navigation is one of the greatest recommendations of this colony. The rivers of Essequibo, Demerara, Berbice, and Corentyn may be navigated inland by schooners or steam-boats, unobstructed, to a distance of from fifty to one hundred and twenty miles, where the rapids and cataracts offer the first impediment to further advance. But as this fertile colony offers so many inducements to settlers, there is every hope, that as the population and cultivation of the interior increase, these impediments may be overcome as easily as those which the St. Lawrence offered to the first settlers in Canada.

A short portage of about seven to eight hundred yards separates the basin of the Amazon from that of the Essequibo. During the rainy season, the river Amazon and the upper Orinoco may be reached from Demerara entirely by inland navigation. So extensive is the water communication of these fertile provinces, that with a little trouble the inland navigation might be extended to Santa Fé de Bogota, and even to the Pacific on the west, and to Buenos Ayres on the south. This is not a visionary scheme: while at the Rio Negro, I met a trader from Matto Grosso who had descended the Madeira with a cargo, which he offered there for sale at the small villages along the Rio Negro. He informed me, that departing from Matto Grosso on the Madeira, they enter the Marmore and its tributary the Guapore, when they drag their canoes about three miles over land to the Aguapeki, which flows in the Jaura and Paraguay. The river Napo offers communication with Quito, the Ucayali with Cuzco, the Huallaga with Lima. Ascending the Rio Negro, and entering the Orinoco by the Cassiquiare, its tributary the Meta offers an uninterrupted navigation to

New Grenada, and within eight miles of Santa Fé de Bogota. Did not British Guiana possess the fertility which is its distinguishing feature, this inland navigation alone would render it of vast importance; but blest as it is with abundant fruitfulness, this extensive water communication heightens its value as a British colony.

Why, then, it may be asked, is Guiana thus stationary in the scale of advancement and emigration? The answer to such a question is simple. Decried with the greatest injustice as unhealthy, no inducement has hitherto been offered to emigrants to select it as the field of their industry and profitable occupation. But if Government were to direct a just share of public attention to this great field for the reception of the surplus population, and its fertility were better known, many would no doubt avail themselves of the advantages which the colony offers. It has been proposed that the land, the title to which has been vested in the Crown, be henceforward sold, and the price applied towards defraying the necessary cost of emigration. This plan has much to recommend it: it has been of immeasurable benefit to Australia, where it has been in operation; and similar advantages might be expected were it extended to Guiana. Lands have been hitherto granted for provisional occupancy or for wood-cutting, but with better prospects for the colony ready purchasers might be easily found*.

Such a measure I am happy to say is now in contemplation. An ordinance has been proposed by Her Majesty's Government to the legislative body of British Guiana, for encouraging the introduction of labourers in husbandry into that colony, and a certain sum is to

* The original price of Crown lands is ten guilders (equal to 14s.) per acre. It is, however, open for competition, and left to the highest bidder.

be appropriated for advancing emigration from Her Majesty's revenue within that colony. Agents are to be appointed beyond the seas, except within the limits of the East Indian company's charter, at any port or place on the western or eastern coasts of the African continent, or at the island of Madagascar. For every able-bodied labourer who lands at British Guiana a certain bounty, according to the average length of the voyage, is to be paid out of the reserved fund; and all labourers, who, on their arrival in the colony, are not immediately provided with the means of employment, shall be provided with wholesome food and convenient lodging on shore, until the means of earning their own subsistence can be procured for them.

Were the exclusive clauses not in existence, the welfare of British Guiana would have been founded upon a firm basis by this ordinance. Still the hope remains that such a desirable boon may yet be granted to the colony.

It is a great mistake to believe that the heat of the climate renders Europeans unable to labour in the tropics. I have seen the Spanish labourers in Puerto Rico working as arduously in the field as the African labourer, although I was told that some of them had only lately arrived from Spain. It is undenied, that the lower classes of Spanish creoles in Puerto Rico undergo exposure to the alternation of rain and sunshine as well as the African creoles, and I am not aware that the Portuguese and Maltese who arrived in Guiana, suffered materially from the climate.

Europeans would be particularly qualified for working in coffee, cocoa, spice, and other plantations, where shady trees protect them against the full influence of the sun; or if their periodical daily labour were restricted to three hours in the morning and two in the afternoon, I have little doubt that they might be employed with advantage, and without danger to their constitutions.

If emigration were made attractive to those ill-rewarded artisans and mechanics, who, with the best inclination to work, are scarcely able to earn a miserable subsistence, they might be induced to emigrate to Guiana, where they would supersede their less skilful competitors, who would have to resort to field labour for subsistence. Cabinet-makers, painters, carpenters, glaziers, shipwrights, rope-makers, coopers, blacksmiths, bricklayers, plumbers, &c. would find profitable employment, and an ample field for their industry.

With the introduction of industrious emigrants from the mother country, and the establishment of colonies in the interior, cultivation will gradually extend, and by this advancement, two points of great importance will be secured; namely, with the spread of civilization, the wealth of the colony must increase; and while those labours which are necessary to reclaim the fertile soil from nature and to make it available, are conducive to the health of those who are thus employed, the example of industrious Europeans must have a high moral influence upon the few aborigines who still inhabit British Guiana; and although the latter may be averse at present to cultivate the coast-lands, I have no doubt they would tender their labour if a colony or settlement were formed in the interior.

Below Aritaka, on either side of the Essequibo, there are districts of no small extent of fertile lands, with extensive forests of excellent timber-trees. The regions between the sand-hills and the first rapids in the river Demerara, those between the Berbice and Corentyn, along the banks of the small river Wicki, the savannahs of which recommend themselves, like those of the Wieroni, as pasture-grounds; the hilly tracts in the vicinity of the first falls in the river Berbice; the fertile regions between the upper Berbice and the river Essequibo in the vicinity of Primoss,—are all well calculated for colonization. The soil is various and highly productive, and the expenses connected with clearing the ground would be repaid by the value of the timber cut down.

The mouth of the Corentyn offers a most eligible situation for the foundation of a township, in the vicinity where at present the plantations Eliza and Mary, and Skeldon are situated. The tract of land south of Skeldon is virgin soil of high fertility. Fears are entertained that the increase of Crab Island will destroy the navigable channel to the port of Berbice: if such an unfortunate event should take place, the Corentyn will be of additional importance.

With the cultivation of these waste tracts, the spiritual and social welfare of the province would spread in equal ratio; and Great Britain will be more than rewarded for the inducement which she may give to emigrants to Guiana. She imports, to the amount of millions, from the Brazils and the United States, articles which might be produced in her own colonies, if the present prejudices of introducing field labourers from the East be overcome and secured by wise regulations. There are boundless regions capable of maintaining thousands of poor beings who are struggling in the East with famine and all the evils in its train. The imports of British manufactures would increase with the population and the prosperity of the colony. Thousands, who in Great Britain depend upon the poor funds for mere subsistence, would in so rich a colony as Guiana become independent, and appear in the list of those who contribute to the consumption of British manufactures, and thus add their share towards the increase of national prosperity.

Guiana bids fair ere long to become a focus of colonization; and with her fertility, her facilities of water communication, she may yet vie with the favoured provinces of the eastern empire, and become, as Sir Walter Raleigh predicted, the El Dorado of Great Britain's possessions in the West.

For Product Safety Concerns and Information please contact our EU representative GPSR@taylorandfrancis.com
Taylor & Francis Verlag GmbH, Kaufingerstraße 24, 80331 München, Germany

www.ingramcontent.com/pod-product-compliance
Lightning Source LLC
Chambersburg PA
CBHW081203240426
43669CB00039B/2793